Fu

Vijaay Kumar Sinha
Rubal Jeet
Meenakshi Jaiswal

Fundamentals of C++ Programming

LAP LAMBERT Academic Publishing

Fundamentals of C++ Programming

By

Vijay Kumar Sinha

Rubaljeet Kaur

Meenakshi Jaiswal

May 2019

Acknowledgements

We express our heartfelt thanks to one and all who contributed and promoted and motivated for this present work. I firstly thanks to our Chandigarh Engineering College, Landran, Mohali for constant support for creative writing. I thank all faculty members of Applied Sciences; especially faculty of PPS. A big thanks to my head of department Dr. Lakhwinder Singh, Dr. Manish Mahajan and the students of CEC, Landran.

We thanks to Lambert Publications for accepting and encouraging our work. At last we thank the almighty for the blessings.

Authors

Vijay Kumar Sinha
Rubaljeet Kaur
Meenakshi Jaiswal   *8 May 2019*

Preface

C++ programming is considered as foundation of computer engineering. By learning C++ students can easily programs for C as well with little effort. This book is aimed for students who is learning C programming with scratch with no any earlier programming base. Its learns C++ programming step by step with self learning approach.

The syllabus includes the syllabus of AICTE new syllabus for B.Tech. BE students of Indian Engineering students as well as world's leading universities.

Whole book is divided into 9 basic chapters. In the back pages we provide a number of practice C programs for students for self practice.

This book is an effort to familiarize the students of all branches in engineering with computer organization, operating systems, problem solving and programming in C++. After the students have successfully completed the course, they shall have sufficient knowledge of the basic computer operations and various programming techniques especially in C++.

We also provide Multiple Choice Questions for competitive exams. We list some solved model question papers for students.

We hope students will definitely found it benifitial and will build a solid base of C++ programming.

We invite learned reader for their valuable comments for further improvements and upliftment of this current edition.

Thanks

Regards

Vijay Kumar Sinha   *Chandigarh Engineering College*

Rubal Jeet   *Landran, Mohali, Punjab.*

Meenakshi   *India*

8/5/2019

Dedicated to

Bjarne Stroustrup

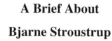

A Brief About

Bjarne Stroustrup

Bjarne Stroustrup born 30 December 1950, is a Danish computer scientist, who is most notable for the creation and development of the C++ programming language. He is a visiting professor at Columbia University, and works at Morgan Stanley as a Managing Director in New York.

Stroustrup has a master's degree in mathematics and computer science (1975) from Aarhus University, Denmark, and a PhD in computer science in 1979 from the University of Cambridge, England[11]supervised by David Wheeler.

Stroustrup began developing C++ in 1979 (then called "C with Classes"), and, in his own words, "invented C++, wrote its early definitions, and produced its first implementation... chose and formulated the design criteria for C++, designed all its major facilities, and was responsible for the processing of extension proposals in the C++ standards committee." Stroustrup also wrote a textbook for the language, *The C++ Programming Language*.

Stroustrup was the head of AT&T Bell Labs' Large-scale Programming Research department, from its creation until late 2002. Stroustrup was elected member of the National Academy of Engineering in 2004. He was elected a Fellow of the Association for Computing Machinery (ACM) in 1994 and the Institute of Electrical and Electronics Engineers (IEEE). From 2002 to 2014, Stroustrup was the College of Engineering Chair in Computer Science Professor at Texas A&M University. As of January 2014, Stroustrup is a Managing Director in the technology division of Morgan Stanley in New York City and a Visiting Professor in Computer Science at Columbia University.

Stroustrup has been a noble doctor at ITMO University since 2013.

Stroustrup won the Senior Dahl–Nygaard Prize in 2015. The same year, he was made a Fellow of the Computer History Museum for his invention of the C++ programming language. In 2017, the Institution of Engineering and Technology (IET) awarded him the Faraday Medal, for pioneering C++, one of the most influential programming languages in the history of computing. On January 3, 2018, Stroustrup was announced as the 2018 winner of the Charles Stark Draper Prize for Engineering, which comes with $500,000. He was named winner of 2018 Computer Pioneer Award of the IEEE Computer Society. He was awarded an honorary doctor from the University Carlos III, Spain on 25 January 2019.

Creation of C++

Bjarne joined the Computing Science Research Center of AT&T Bell Laboratories in 1979. Strongly influenced by the object-oriented model of the SIMULA language (created by Dahl and Nygaard!), he began work on developing class extensions to the C Language so that developers could write software using a far higher level of abstraction and sophistication while retaining the efficiency of C.

Bjarne said "My initial aim for C++ was a language where I could write programs that were as elegant as Simula programs, yet as efficient as C programs."[2] The first C++ language reference manual was published internally in 1984, and the C++ language was released commercially in 1985. C++ spread rapidly and became the dominant object-oriented programming language in the 1990s. The language remains one of the most widely used programming languages today.

A Short Summary of Stroustrup's Career

Bjarne Stroustrup received his PhD from the University of Aarhus in 1979, and joined the famed 1127 computing sciences center, the birthplace of Unix and C, at Bell Labs in Murray Hill. The open, flexible research atmosphere encouraged him to consider adapting concepts from Simula, which he had used in his Ph.D. thesis work, to C. He is quoted as saying: "When I joined, I was basically told to do 'something interesting...'"

After AT&T split up in 1996 into AT&T and Lucent, Stroustrup stayed with AT&T and was a founding member of AT&T Labs, where he was the head of the Large-Scale Programming Research Department until 2002. He then moved to the computer science department of Texas A&M. He is currently also a Managing Director in the Technology Division of Morgan Stanley.

During the three decades since the release of C++, Stroustrup has published over 100 papers related to C++ and several books on C++ that have been translated into multiple languages. He has received numerous awards and honorary degrees, including the ACM's Grace Hopper Award, election to the National Academy of Engineering, IEEE Fellow, Bell Labs Fellow, and AT&T Fellow.

C++ Popularity

According to Stroustrup, "C and C++ became popular because they were flexible, cheap, and more efficient than alternatives. C owes much of its initial popularity to the popularity of Unix. C++ owes much of its initial popularity to its high degree of compatibility with C." He reminds us that "both C and C++ were invented in the Computer Science Research Center of Bell Labs in Murray Hill and found their initial serious use within Bell Labs and AT&T."

Legacy of C and C++

C and C++, remarkably, remain two of the most widely used programming languages today and have influenced other languages, such as Java. Systems software, large-scale data processing systems, networking software and the like are programmed in C++; as an example, the well-known MapReduce library at Google was created with C++. At Bell Labs, C++ continues to be used in a number of projects ranging from networking research to formal verification.

A Brief About
Dennis MacAlistair Ritchie

Father of C Programming

Dennis MacAlistair Ritchie was a renowned American computer scientist, best remembered for creating the "C" computer programming language and his contributions to the development of UNIX Operating System. He was born in Bronxville, New York in 1941. His father, Alistair Ritchie, was a scientist at Bell Labs and wrote a book on circuit theory. Ritchie's family moved to New Jersey when he was a child. There he studied at Summit High School and later obtained a BS degree in Physics in 1963 and a Ph.D. in Applied Mathematics in 1967, both from Harvard University.

Ritchie and his associate Ken Thompson worked together at AT&T Bell Labs to create the Unix Computer Operating System. This is one of the two most significant achievements of Ritchie's career, the other being the development of the C Programming Language. C was the descendant of the B programming language developed by Bell Labs. It was meant to be a "higher level" computer language and was the basis on which the UNIX Operating System was run. Thompson and Ritchie gained tremendous success with UNIX and the C Language. Before C, there was hardly any standardization in the computer industry. Computer programs were very specific to a particular type of hardware and could not be run on just any computer. UNIX and C served to combine and standardize the scattered bits and piece of software in the industry.

C was a powerful, multi-purpose language and combined with UNIX, their widespread impact and influence is evident in almost every aspect of the computing industry today. For instance, languages which came later (such as Java and C++) were derived from the C language, browser codes are all written in C, and the UNIX kernel (an important basis on which is the internet works) is also written in C. Even Microsoft Windows was initially written in C. Both of Apple Inc's Operating Systems (called iOS and MAC OS X) are based on the UNIX system. There is no doubt about the impact of Ritchie's contributions on the computing industry and the world. It would be fair to say that he has significantly altered the course of the computing industry's history.

As the popularity of the C language rose, the use of C and UNIX spread throughout the industry and it began to be taught to computer engineers in universities. This was in large part due to the success of Kerninghan and Ritchie's book titled "The C Programming Language". This book was published in 1978, and served as a comprehensive manual for learning how to use C. The book's authors are often collectively referred to as "K & R". This book was so successful that it's been translated into 20 different languages. It's popularity is due to the fact that it's easy to use and understand.

When AT&T was restructured, Ritchie was transferred to a newly created division called Lucent Technologies, where he worked until his retirement in 2007 as Head of System Software Research Department. Ritchie's list of awards and accolades is extensive. He is a Fellow of the Computer History Museum, and recipient of the National Medal of Technology from President Bill Clinton, Achievement Award by the Industrial Research Institute and the Japan Prize for Information and Communications.

By nature, Dennis Ritchie was a humble, polite and well liked person. He looked like a typical IT guru with long hair and a beard. He preferred to start working around noon and went home and worked into the late hours of the night. Ritchie suffered from poor health for the last few years of his life and died in October 2011 at the age of 70. His legacy lives on in the form of the prevalent application of his contributions to modern computing.

AT&T Bell Laboratories

In 1880, when the French government awarded Alexander Graham Bell the Volta Prize of 50,000 francs (approximately US$10,000 at that time; about $270,000 in current dollars) for the invention of the telephone, he used the award to fund the Volta Laboratory (*Alexander Graham Bell Laboratory*) in Washington, D.C. in collaboration with Sumner Tainter and Bell's cousin Chichester Bell.[2] The laboratory was variously known as the *Volta Bureau*, the *Bell Carriage House*, the *Bell Laboratory* and the *Volta Laboratory*.

It focused on the analysis, recording, and transmission of sound. Bell used his considerable profits from the laboratory for further research and education to permit the " diffusion of knowledge relating to the deaf": resulting in the founding of the Volta Bureau (c. 1887) which was located at Bell's father's house at 1527 35th Street N.W. in Washington, D.C. Its carriage house became their headquarters in 1889.

In 1893, Bell constructed a new building close by at 1537 35th Street N.W., specifically to house the lab. This building was declared a National Historic Landmark in 1972.

After the invention of the telephone, Bell maintained a relatively distant role with the Bell System as a whole, but continued to pursue his own personal research interests.

Nokia Bell Labs (formerly named **AT&T Bell Laboratories** and **Bell Telephone Laboratories**) is an industrial research and scientific development company owned by Finnish company Nokia. Its headquarters are located in Murray Hill, New Jersey. Other laboratories are located around the world (with some in the United States). Bell Labs has its origins in the complex past of the Bell System.

In the late 19th century, the laboratory began as the Western Electric Engineering Department and was located at 463 West Street in New York City. In 1925, after years of conducting research and development under Western Electric, the Engineering Department was reformed into Bell Telephone Laboratories and under the shared ownership of American Telephone & Telegraph Companyand Western Electric.

Researchers working at Bell Labs are credited with the development of radio astronomy, the transistor, the laser, the photovoltaic cell, the charge-coupled device (CCD), information theory, the Unix operating system, and the programming languages C, C++, and S. Nine Nobel Prizes have been awarded for work completed at Bell Laboratories.

Alexander Graham Bell : Founder of AT & T Bells Lab

Alexander Graham Bell (March 3, 1847 – August 2, 1922) was a Scottish-born scientist, inventor, engineer, and innovator who is credited with inventing and patenting the first practical telephone. He also founded the American Telephone and Telegraph Company (AT&T) in 1885.

Bell's father, grandfather, and brother had all been associated with work on elocution and speech and both his mother and wife were deaf, profoundly influencing Bell's life's work.[8] His research on hearing and speech further led him to experiment with hearing devices which eventually culminated in Bell being awarded the first U.S. patent for the telephone in 1876. Bell considered his invention an intrusion on his real work as a scientist and refused to have a telephone in his study.

Many other inventions marked Bell's later life, including groundbreaking work in optical telecommunications, hydrofoils, and aeronautics. Although Bell was not one of the 33 founders of the National Geographic Society, he had a strong influence on the magazine while serving as the second president from January 7, 1898, until 1903.

Contents

Detailed Contents

1. Overview of C++ Language : Introduction to C++ language, structure of a C++ program, concepts of compiling and linking, IDE and its features; Basic terminology - Character set, tokens, identifiers, keywords, fundamental data types, literal and symbolic constants, declaring variables, initializing variables, type modifiers.

2. Operators and expressions: Operators in C++, precedence and associativity of operators, expressions and their evaluation, type conversions.

3. Beginning with C++ program: Input/output using extraction (>>) and insertion (<<) operators, writing simple C++ programs, comments in C++, stages of program execution.

4. Control Structures: Decision making statements: if, nested if, if – else. Else if ladder, switch, Loops and iteration: while loop, for loop, do – while loop, nesting of loops, break statement, continue statement, goto statement, use of control structures through illustrative programming examples.

5. Functions : Advantages of using functions, structure of a function, declaring and defining functions, return statement, formal and actual arguments, const argument, default arguments, concept of reference variable, call by value, call by reference, library functions, recursion, storage classes. Use of functions through illustrative programming examples.

6. Arrays and Strings: Declaration of arrays, initialization of array, accessing elements of array, I/O of arrays, passing arrays as arguments to a function, multidimensional arrays. String as array of characters, initializing string variables, I / O of strings, string manipulation functions (strlen, strcat, strcpy, strcmp), passing strings to a function. Use of arrays and strings through illustrative programming examples

7. Concepts of Object Oriented Programming: Introduction to Classes, Objects, Data abstraction, Data encapsulation, inheritance and polymorphism.

8. Classes and Objects: Defining classes and declaring objects, public and private keywords, constructors and destructors, defining member functions inside and outside of a class, accessing members of a class, friend function. Use of classes and objects through illustrative programming examples.

9. Basics of File Handling: Opening, reading, and writing of files, error handling during files operation.

Suggested Readings/ Books

1. E. Balagurusamy, Object-Oriented Programming with C++, Tata McGraw Hill.

2. Lafore R., Object Oriented Programming in C++, Waite Group.

3. Bjarne Stroustrup, The C++ Programming Language, Addison Wesley.

4. Lippman F. B, C++ Primer, Addison Wesley.

5. R. S. Salaria, Computer Concepts and Programming in C++, Salaria Publishing House.

6. Gurvinder Singh, Krishan Saluja, Fundamentals of Computer Programming & IT,   Kalyani Publishers.

7. R. S. Salaria, Fundamentals of Computers, Salaria Publishing House.

Chapter 1 : Overview of C++ language

Introduction : C++ was developed at AT & T Bell Laboratories in 1930'sby 'Bjarne Stroustrup'. He called C++ as "C with classes". 'C++' name was coined by "Rick Mascitti".

	Bjarne Stroustrup was born in Aarhus, Denmark, in 1950. He received a master's in mathematics from Aarhus University in 1975 and a PhD in computer science from Cambridge University in 1979.
Design and programming are human activities; forget that and all is lost. *-Bjarne Stroustrup*	Stroustrup then joined Bell Labs' Computer Science Research Center in Murray Hill, New Jersey, where he designed and implemented C++. This language, based on C and inspired by Simula, provides a set of general and flexible abstraction mechanisms that can be mapped directly and efficiently onto computer hardware. C++ revolutionized the software industry by enabling a variety of software development techniques-including object-oriented programming, generic programming, and general resource management-to be deployed at scale. For more than two decades, C++ has been among the most widely used programming languages, with applications in areas including general systems programming, communications, computer graphics, games, user-interfaces, embedded systems, financial systems, avionics, and scientific computation. The influence of C++ and the ideas it pioneered and popularized are clearly visible far beyond the C++ community.

 **Dennis Ritchie**, the man behind the scenes who create the **"C"** programming language or as they call him **"Father of the C programming language"**. Richie was born on September 9, 1941 in Bronxville, New York. His father **Alistair Ritchie**, was a switching systems engineer at **Bell Laboratories**.

Dennis was later moved to Summit, New Jersey with his family. Dennis graduated from Summit High School, then got a bachelors degree from Harvard University in Physics and Applied Mathematics field in 1963, and a PhD in Mathematics in 1968 from Harvard University. He moved later to the Massachusetts Institute of Technology.

Dennis is a key developer of the UNIX operating system, and co-author of the book **"The C Programming Language"**. He worked along with Ken Thompson (A scientist who wrote the original UNIX). Later he developed a collaboration on the C programming language with Brian Kernighan and they were known together as K&R (Kernighan & Ritchie). Dennis Ritchie had an important contribution to UNIX which was that UNIX ported to different machines and platforms. His ideas still live on, at the center of modern operating systems design, in almost all new programming languages, and in every bit of open systems.

C++ Character Set : It is set of valid characters that a language can recognize. A character represents any letters, digits or any other sign.

Letters : A – Z , a – z

Digits : 0 – 9

Special Symbols : Space, +, -, *, /, ^, \, ( ), { }, [ ], =, !=, <, >, .,, ", ', $ etc

White Space : Blank space, Horizontal Tab (→), Carriage return, New line, Form feed.

Other Character : 256 ASCII characters

Tokens (Lexical units) : In a passage of test, individual words and punctuation marks are called tokens or lexical units or Lexical elements.

The smallest individual unit in a program is known as a token or a lexical unit.

C++ has the following token :

- Keywords
- Punctuators
- Identifiers
- Operators
- Literals (constants)

Keywords : Keywords have special meaning to the language compiler. These are reserved for special purpose e.g break, case, class, char, new etc.

Punctuators (Seperators) : [ ], ( ), { }, , , ; , : , *, ...=, # etc

Identifiers : An Identifier is and arbitrarily long sequence of letters or/and digets and are used as the general terminology for the names given to different parts of the program viz variables, objects, classes, function, array ets.

Rules for defining Identifiers:

- An identifier can consist of alphabets, digits and/or underscores.
- It must not start with a digit
- C++ is case sensitive that is upper case and lower case letters are considered different from each other.
- It should not be a reserved word.

Operators :

Operator Name	Associativity	Operators
Primary scope resolution	left to right	::
Primary	left to right	() [ ] . -> **dynamic_cast typeid**
Unary	right to left	++ -- + - ! ~ & * (*type_name*) **sizeof new delete**
C++ Pointer to Member	left to right	.*->*
Multiplicative	left to right	* / %
Additive	left to right	+ -
Bitwise Shift	left to right	<< >>
Relational	left to right	< > <= >=

Equality	left to right	== !=
Bitwise AND	left to right	&
Bitwise Exclusive OR	left to right	^
Bitwise Inclusive OR	left to right	|
Logical AND	left to right	&&
Logical OR	left to right	||
Conditional	right to left	? :
Assignment	right to left	= += -= *= /= <<= >>= %= &= ^= |=
Comma	left to right	,

Literals (Constants) : These are data items that never change their value during a program run.

- Integer Constant

- Character Constant

- Floating Constant

- String Constant

First Look at C++ Program

    // First program

#include<iostream.h>

Int main( )

{

Cout<<"Welcome to C++ program";

return 0;

}

// : for comments

 # : directives for preprocessor. So, these statements are processed before compilation take place

#include<iostream.h> statement tells the compiler processor to include the header file iostream.

Int main( ) : this line indicates beginning of main function. The content of main( ) is always the first to be executed when a program starts.

Cout : It is standard output stream and insert a sequence of characters " "

Every excutable statement in C++ is terminated by a semicolon (;)

Structure of C++

Include files
Class declaration
Member function definition
Main function program

Compiling & Linking

Turbo C++

- File can be created and saved from file option and editing by edit option
- Compilation is done under Compile option
- Execution under Run Option

Fundamental Data Types:

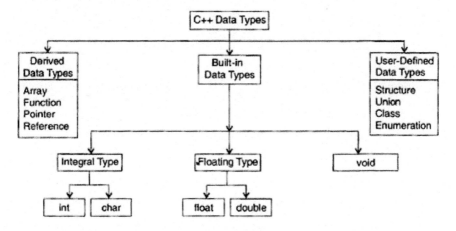

Data types are means to identify the type of data and associated operations of handling it

I.   Fundamental (Built in)

II.   Derived (user defined)

Int (integers) : Whole numbers, -32768 to 32767

Int Datatype Modifiers	Approximate Size (In Bytes)	Minimal Range
Short	2	-32768 to 32767
Unsigned Short	2	0 to 65,535
Signed short	2	Same as short
Int	2	Same as short
Unsigned int	2	Same as unsigned short
Signed int	2	Same as int
Long	4	-2,147,483,648 to 2,147,483,647
Unsigned long	4	0 to 4,294,967,295
Signed long	4	Same as long

Character datatype Modifiers

Character Datatype Modifiers	Approximate Size (In Bytes)	Minimal Range
Char or Signed Char	1	-128 to 127
Unsigned char	1	0 to 255

Floating Point Data type Modifiers

Float Datatype Modifiers	Approximate Size (In Bytes)	Minimal Range	Digits of precision
Float	4	$3.4*10^38$ to $3.4*10^38-1$	7
Double	8	$1.7*10^-308$ to $1.7*10^308-1$	15
Long double	10	$3.4*10-4932$ to $1.1*104932-1$	19

Variables : It represents named storage locations whose value can be manipulated during program run.

Syntax for variable declaration :

Data_type variable_name;

e.g   int I;
           float f;
           char c;

initialization of variable :   int val = 1001;
dynamic initialization :   float avg;
                                avg = sum/count; or float ave = sum/count;

Multiple Choice Questions

1. The symbol shown in the Figure in flow chart represents

(A) In-connector

(B) Out-connector

(C) Output

(D) End.

2. The symbol shown in Figure in flow chart represents

(A) In connector

(B) Out connector

(C) Annotation

(D) Input/output.

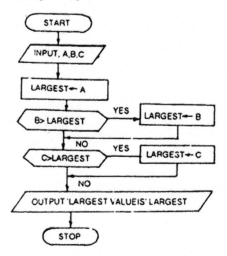

3. The problem represented by the flow chart is

(A) To compare A, B and C

(B) To find lowest of A, B and C

(C) To find average of A,B and C

(D) To find largest value of A, B and C

4. The output will be

(A) Stop

(B) Average number

(C) Largest number

(D) Least number.

5.Which operator is having the highest precedence?
a) postfix
b) unary
c) shift
d) equality

 6.What is this operator called ?: ?
a) conditional
b) relational
c) casting operator
d) none of the mentioned

7. What is the size of wchar_t in C++?
a) 2
b) 4
c) 2 or 4
d) based on the number of bits in the system

8. Pick the odd one out
a) array type
b) character type
c) boolean type
d) integer type

9. Which datatype is used to represent the absence of parameters?
a) int
b) short
c) void
d) float

10. The constants are also called as
a) const
b) preprocessor

c) literals

d) none of the mentioned

11. How the constants are declared?

a) const keyword

b) #define preprocessor

c) both a and b

d) None of the mentioned

12. Which of the following will not return a value?

a) null

b) void

c) empty

d) free

13. What does the following statement mean?
   void a;

a) variable a is of type void

b) a is an object of type void

c) declares a variable with value a

d) flags an error

15. Choose the incorrect option

a) void is used when the function does not return a value.

b) void is also used when the value of a pointer is null.

c) void is used as the base type for pointers to objects of unknown type.

d) void is a special fundamental type.

16. File manipulation functions in C++ are available in which <u>header file</u>?

A) streams.h

B) stdio.h

C) stdlib.h

D) files.h

17. A variable is defined within a block in a body of a function. Which of the following are true?

A) It is visible throughout the function.

B) It is visible from the point of definition to the end of the program.

C) It is visible from the point of definition to the end of the block.

D) It is visible throughout the block.

18. Which of the following statement is not true about preprocessor directives?

a. These are lines read and processed by the preprocessor

b. They do not produce any code by themselves

c. These must be written on their own line

d. They end with a semicolon

19. Regarding following statement which of the statements is true?
   constint a = 100;

a. Declares a variable a with 100 as its initial value

b. Declares a construction a with 100 as its initial value

c. Declares a constant a whose value will be 100

d. Constructs an integer type variable with a as identifier and 100 as value

20. How to declare a wide character in string literal?

a) L prefix

b) l prefix

c) W prefix

d) none of the mentioned

Chapter-2 : Operators and Expressions

Operators in C++:

An operator is a symbol that tells the compiler to perform specific mathematical or logical manipulations. Operations are represented by operators and the objects of the operations are referred as operands.

C++ is rich in built-in operators and provides the following types of operators:

- Arithmetic Operators
- Relational Operators
- Logical Operators
- Bitwise Operators
- Assignment Operators
- Misc Operators

Arithmetic Operators: There are following arithmetic operators supported by C++ language:

Assume variable A holds 10 and variable B holds 20, then:

Operator	Description	Example
+	Adds two operands	A + B will give 30
-	Subtracts second operand from the first	A - B will give -10
*	Multiplies both operands	A * B will give 200
/	Divides numerator by de-numerator	B / A will give 2
%	Modulus Operator and remainder of after an integer division	B % A will give 0
++ (Increment)	Increment operator, increases integer value by one	A++ will give 11
-- (Decrement)	Decrement operator, decreases integer value by one	A-- will give 9

Relational Operators: There are following relational operators supported by C++ language

Assume variable A holds 10 and variable B holds 20, then:

Operator	Description	Example
==	Checks if the values of two operands are equal or not, if yes then condition becomes true.	(A == B) is not true.
!=	Checks if the values of two operands are equal or not, if values are not equal then condition becomes true.	(A != B) is true.
>	Checks if the value of left operand is greater than the value of right operand, if yes then condition becomes true.	(A > B) is not true.
<	Checks if the value of left operand is less than the value of right operand, if yes then condition becomes true.	(A < B) is true.
>=	Checks if the value of left operand is greater than or equal to the value of right operand, if yes then condition becomes true.	(A >= B) is not true.
<=	Checks if the value of left operand is less than or equal to the value of right operand, if yes then condition becomes true.	(A <= B) is true.

Logical Operators: There are following logical operators supported by C++ language.

Assume variable A holds 1 and variable B holds 0, then:

Operator	Description	Example
&&	Called Logical AND operator. If both the operands are non-zero, then condition becomes true.	(A && B) is false.
‖	Called Logical OR Operator. If any of the two operands is non-zero, then condition becomes true.	(A ‖ B) is true.
!	Called Logical NOT Operator. Use to reverses the logical state of its operand. If a condition is true, then Logical NOT operator will make false.	!(A && B) is true.

Assignment Operators: There are following assignment operators supported by C++ language:

Operator	Description	Example
=	Simple assignment operator, Assigns values from right side operands to left side operand	C = A + B will assign value of A + B into C
+=	Add AND assignment operator, It adds right operand to the left operand and assign the result to left operand	C += A is equivalent to C = C + A

-=	Subtract AND assignment operator, It subtracts right operand from the left operand and assign the result to left operand	C -= A is equivalent to C = C - A
*=	Multiply AND assignment operator, It multiplies right operand with the left operand and assign the result to left operand	C *= A is equivalent to C = C * A
/=	Divide AND assignment operator, It divides left operand with the right operand and assign the result to left operand	C /= A is equivalent to C = C / A
%=	Modulus AND assignment operator, It takes modulus using two operands and assign the result to left operand	C %= A is equivalent to C = C % A
<<=	Left shift AND assignment operator	C <<= 2 is same as C = C << 2
>>=	Right shift AND assignment operator	C >>= 2 is same as C = C >> 2
&=	Bitwise AND assignment operator	C &= 2 is same as C = C & 2
^=	bitwise exclusive OR and assignment operator	C ^= 2 is same as C = C ^ 2
|=	bitwise inclusive OR and assignment operator	C |= 2 is same as C = C | 2

Miscellaneous Operators: There are few other operators supported by C++ Language.

Operator	Description
sizeof	sizeof operator returns the size of a variable. For example, sizeof(a), where a is integer, will return 4.
Condition? X : Y	Conditional operator. If Condition is true ? then it returns value X : otherwise value Y
,	Comma operator causes a sequence of operations to be performed. The value of the entire comma expression is the value of the last expression of the comma-separated list.
. (dot) and -> (arrow)	Member operators are used to reference individual members of classes, structures, and unions.
Cast	Casting operators convert one data type to another. For example, int(2.2000) would return 2.
&	Pointer operator & returns the address of an variable. For example &a; will give actual address of the variable.
*	Pointer operator * is pointer to a variable. For example *var; will pointer to a variable var.

Precedence and Associativity of Operators:

Operator precedence determines the grouping of terms in an expression. This affects how an expression is evaluated. Certain operators have higher precedence than others; for example, the multiplication operator has higher precedence than the addition operator:

For example x = 7 + 3 * 2; here, x is assigned 13, not 20 because operator * has higher precedence than +, so it first gets multiplied with 3*2 and then adds into 7.

Category	Operator	Associativity
Postfix	() [] -> . ++ - -	Left to right
Unary	+ - ! ~ ++ - - (type)* & sizeof	Right to left
Multiplicative	* / %	Left to right
Additive	+ -	Left to right
Shift	<< >>	Left to right
Relational	< <= > >=	Left to right
Equality	== !=	Left to right
Bitwise AND	&	Left to right
Bitwise XOR	^	Left to right
Bitwise OR	|	Left to right
Logical AND	&&	Left to right
Logical OR	||	Left to right
Conditional	?:	Right to left
Assignment	= += -= *= /= %=>>= <<= &= ^= |=	Right to left
Comma	,	Left to right

Expressions and their Evaluation:

Expression in C++ is form when we combine operands (variables and constant) and C++ operators.

Expression can also be defined as a combination of Operands and Operators.

Operands in C++ program are those values on which we want to perform operation.

There are three types of expressions:

1. Arithmetic expression

2. Relational expression

3. Logical expression

Evaluate the expression: Let int a, mb=2, k=4

a= mb*3/4+k/4+8-mb+5/8

  = (2*3)/4+4/4+8-2+5/8

  = 6/4+1+8-2+5/8

  = 1+1+8-2+0

  = 10-2

  = 8

Type Conversions:

When constant and variables of different types are mixed in an expression they are converted to the same type. The process of converting one predefined type into another is called type conversion.

There are two types of Type Conversion:

1. Implicit Type Conversion
2. Explicit Type Conversion

Implicit Type Conversion: It is a conversion performed by the compiler without programmer's intervention. The C++ compiler converts all operands up to the type of the largest operand which is called type promotion.

Explicit Type Conversion: An explicit type conversion is user defined that forces an expression to be of specific type. The explicit conversion of an operand to a specific type is called type casting.

Multiple Choice Questions

OPRATORS and EXPRESSIONS

1. **Which operator is having the highest precedence?**
    a) postfix
    b) unary
    c) shift
    d) equality

2. **What is this operator called ? : ?**
    a) **conditional**
    b) relational
    c) casting operator
    d) none of the mentioned

3. **What is the output of this program?**
```
#include<iostream.h>
int main()
{
int a;
a = 5 + 3 * 5;
cout << a;
return 0;
}
```
    a) 35
    b) **20**
    c) 25
    d) 30

4. **What is the output of this program?**
```
#include < iostream.h >
int main()
{
int i, j;
j = 10;
i = (j++, j + 100, 999 + j);
cout << i;
return 0;
}
```
    a)   1000
    b)   11
    c)   1010
    d)   1001

5.   In C++ .... operator is used for Dynamic memory allocation.

a) Scope resolution

b) Conditional

c) New

d) Membership access

6.   The if..else statement can be replaced by which operator?

a)   Bitwise operator

b)   **Conditional operator**

c)   Multiplicative operator

d)   none of the mentioned

7.   Which of the following is the correct operator to compare two variables?

a)   :=

b)   =

c)   equal

d)   ==

8.   Which of the following is the boolean operator for logical-and?

a)   &

b)   &&

c) |

d) |&

9.   The precedence of arithmetic operators is (from highest to lowest)

a) $\%, *, /, +, -$

b) $\%, +, /, *, -$

c) $+, -, \%, *, /$

d) $\%, +, -, *, /$

10.   Which of the following data type will throw an error on modulus operation ($\%$)?

a) char

b) short

c) int

d) float

11.   Result of a logical or relational expression in C++ is

a) True or False

b) 0 or 1

c) 0 if expression is false and any positive number if expression is true

d) None of the mentioned

12.   Which among the following is NOT a logical or relational operator?

a) !=

b) ==

c) ||

d) =

13.   Relational operators cannot be used on:

a) structure

b) long

c) strings

d) float

14.   When double is converted to float, the value is?

a) Truncated

b) Rounded

c) Depends on the compiler

d) Depends on the standard

15.   What is the output of this C++ code?

```
#include <iostream.h>
int main()
{
  int a = 1, b = 1, c;
  c = a++ + b;
  Cout<<a<<b;
}
```

a = 1, b = 1

b) a = 2, b = 1

c) a = 1, b = 2

d) a = 2, b = 2

16.   When do you need to use type-conversions?

a) The value to be stored is beyond the max limit

b) The value to be stored is in a form not supported by that data type

c) To reduce the memory in use, relevant to the value

d) All of the mentioned

17.   What is the output of this C++ code?

```
#include <iostream.h>
int main()
{
int x = 1, y = 0;
x &&= y;
      Cout<<x;

}
```

a)   **Compile time error**

b)   1

c)   0

d)   Undefined behavior

18.   **What is the type of the below assignment expression if x is of type float, y is of type int?**

   y = x + y;

a) int

b) float

c) There is no type for an assignment expression

d) double

19.   **To increase the value of c by one, which of the following is wrong?**

a) c++;

b) c=c+1;

c) c+1=>c;

d) c+=1;

20.   **What is the output of this program?**

```
#include <iostream.h>
int main()
{
    int a = 5, b = 6, c, d;
    c = a, b;
    d = (a, b);
    cout << c << ' ' << d;
    return 0;
}
```

a)   **5 6**

b) 6 5

c) 6 7

d) none of the mentioned

Chapter- 3 : Beginning with C++ program

Introduction to C++:

C++ was developed by Bjarne Stroustrup of AT&T Bell Laboratories in the early 1980's, and is based on the C language. The "++" is a syntactic construct used in C (to increment a variable), and C++ is intended as an incremental improvement of C. Most of C is a subset of C++, so that most C programs can be compiled (i.e. converted into a series of low-level instructions that the computer can execute directly) using a C++ compiler.

Input/output using extraction (>>) and insertion (<<) operators:

*   Input coming from user's terminal referred as standard input is tied to predefined iostream cin. Input operator is known as extraction operator and the symbol used for cin is >>.

*   Output directed to user's terminal referred as standard output is tied to the predefined iostream cout. Output operator is known as insertion operator and the symbol used for cout is <<.

Writing simple C++ programs:

Basic Syntax and Structure of C++ program:

A C++ program can be developed from a basic structure. The general structure of C++ program with classes is as shown below (which is also called overview of a C++ program):

1. Documentation Section

2. Preprocessor Directives or Compiler Directives Section

3. Main C++ program function called main ( )

4. Beginning of the program: Left brace {

5. End of the main program: Right brace}

1. **Documentation Section**: In Documentation section we give the Heading and Comments. Comment statement is the non-executable statement.

Comment can be given in two ways:

*   **Single Line Comment**: Comment can be given in single line by using *"II"*.

    The general syntax is: // Single Text line

    For Example: *II* Add Two Numbers (Heading of the program)

*   **Multiple Line Comment:** Comment can be given in multiple lines starting by using "/*" and end with "*/".

    The general syntax is: /* Text Line 1

                             Text Line 2

                             Text Line 3 */

For Example: /* Write a C++ program to find the sum and average of five numbers. */

2. **Preprocessor Directives:** Lines beginning with a hash sign (#) are directives read and interpreted by what is known as the preprocessor. They are special lines interpreted before the compilation of the program itself begins. In this case, the directive #include <iostream.h>, instructs the preprocessor to include a section of standard C++ code, known as header iostream, that allows to perform standard input and output operations.

3. **Main C++ program function called main ( ):** Every C++ program must have a main function to start execution. If main function is not present in a C++ program then the code will not be executed. There are many formats of main function but we usually use void main (). A pair of parenthesis is required after main word. It can be empty or may have some parameters as well. The keyword "void" has its own significance. Currently it means that main function is not returning any value to the operating system.

4. **Beginning of the program (Left brace {):** Every function including main function must start with curly bracket. We can say that body of the function is written between the pair of curly brackets.

5. **End of the main program (Right brace}):** Every function including main function must ends with curly bracket.

Basic example of C++ program:

```
#include <iostream.h>
#include <conio.h>
void main()
{
cout << "Hello this is C++";
}
```

Output: Hello this is C++

Stages of Program Execution: (Program Development Life Cycle)

It is a systematic way of developing a program. The PDCL process is divided into following 6 phases:

1. Define the problem

2. Design the problem

3. Build the program

4. Testing the program

5. Executing the program

6. Maintaining the program

1. **Define the problem:** It is the first step of PDCL. In this we have to define the problem in detail.

2. **Design the problem:** In designing section of problem we will create the algorithm, flowchart, pseudo code of the program.

3. **Build the program:** After the designing of a program a programmer will create a source code of the problem. A source code is the code that is understood by the compiler.

4. **Testing the program:** After creating a source code it will be tested for the bugs or errors. If there is an error then it should be removed to execute the program.

5. **Executing the program:** After removing an error in source code the program will be executed for desired output.

6. **Maintaining the program:** Program should be maintained for the future use.

Program Development Life Cycle:

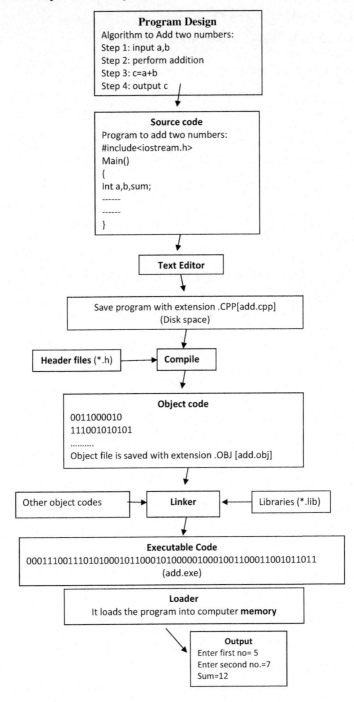

Multiple Choice Questions

BEGINNING WITH C++ PROGRAM

1.   Which of the following is a correct comment?
a)   */ Comments */
b)   ** Comment **
c)   /* Comment */
d)   { Comment }

2.   What punctuation ends most lines of C++ code?
a)   . (dot)
b)   ; (semi-colon)
c)   : (colon)
d)   ' (single quote)

3.   What is the only function all C++ programs must contain?
a)   start()
b)   system()
c)   **main()**
d)   program()

4.   What punctuation is used to signal the beginning and end of code blocks?
a)   { }
b)   -> and <-
c)   BEGIN and END
d)   (and)

5.   Which header file is used with input and output operations   in C++?
a) stdio.h
b) cstdio
c) iostream
d) None of the mentioned

6.   Which will be used with physical devices to interact from C++ program?
a) Programs
b) Library
c) Streams
d) None of the mentioned

7.   How many indicators are available in c++?
a) 4
b) 3

c) 2
d) 1
Explanation:There are three indicators are available in C++. They are Error indicator, End-Of-File indicator and Position indicator.

8.   **Which operator is used for input stream?**
a) >
b) >>
c) <
d) <<

9.   **Where does a cin stops it extraction of data?**
a) By seeing a blankspace
b) By seeing (
c) Both a & b
d) None of the mentioned
Explanation: cin will stop its extraction when it encounters a blank space.

10.   **What is a comment in c++?**
a) comments are parts of the source code disregarded by the compiler
b) comments are executed by compiler to find the meaning of the comment
c) comments are executable
d) none of the mentioned

11.   **What type of comments does c++ support?**
a) single line
b) multi line
c) single line and multi line
d) none of the mentioned

12.   **What is meant by ofstream in c++?**
a) write to a file
b) Reads from a file
c) Both a & b
d) None of the mentioned

13. **Which of the following is not a C++ Compiler ?**
a)C front
b) Turbo C++
c) Borland C++
d) C++ compiler

14.   **In CPP, it is mandatory and must to initialize const variables.**
a. True
b. False

15. What is the size of an int data type?
a) 4 Bytes
b) 8 Bytes
c) Depends on the system/compiler
d) Cannot be determined.

16. #include <iostream.h> is called
a) Preprocessor directive
b) Inclusion directive
c) File inclusion directive
d) None of the mentioned

17. C ++ preprocessor is conceptually the first step during compilation
a) true
b) false
c) Depends on the compiler
d) Depends on the standard

18. A preprocessor is a program
a) That processes its input data to produce output that is used as input to another program
b) That is nothing but a loader
c) That links various source files
d) All of the mentioned

19. The preprocessor provides the ability for _____.
a) The inclusion of header files
b) The inclusion of macro expansions
c) Conditional compilation and line control.
d) All of the mentioned

20. Which of the following is not a valid C variable name?
a) int number;
b) float rate;
c) int variable_count;
d) int $main;

Chapter 4 : Control Structure

Decision making statements:-

- **If- statement**:- The ability to control the flow of your program, letting it make decisions on what code to execute, is valuable to the programmer. The if statement allows you to control if a program enters a section of code or not based on whether a given condition is true or false.

Syntax:- if(expression)
            Statements;
Example:-
                Char ch;
                Cin>>ch;
                If(ch==' ')
                Cout<<"you have entered a space"<<"\n";
If(ch>='0'&&ch<='9')
Cout<<"you have entered a digit"<<"\n";

- **If-else statement**:- An **if** statement can be followed by an optional **else** statement, which executes when the Boolean expression is false.
            Syntax:- if(expression)
                Statement 1;
                Else
                Statement 2;
                Example:- int I;
                Cin>>I;
                If(I%2==0)
                Print("even");
                Else
                Print("odd)

- **Nested-ifs**: means you can use one if or else if statement inside another if or else if statement(s).
                Syntax:-1.   if(exp1)
                    {
                    If(exp2)
                    Statement 1;

Else
Statement 2;
}
2.   if(exp1)
Body of if;
Else
{
If(exp2)
Stmt 1;
Else
Stmt 2;
}

3.   if(exp1)
Stmt 1;
Else if(exp2)
Stmt 2;
Else if(exp3)
Stmt 3;
:

:

Else
Stmt n;

Example:-
Int main()
{
Char ch;
If(ch>=48 && ch<=57)
Cout<<"digit entered");
Else if(ch>=65 && ch<=90)
Cout<<"uppercase character";
Else if(ch>=97 && ch<=122)
Cout<<"lowercase character";
Else
Cout<<"special character";
Return 0;
}

• **Switch statement**:- a switch statement is a type of selection control mechanism used to allow the value of a variable or expression to change the control flow of program execution via a multiway branch.

Syntax:-
Switch(expression)
{
Case const1: stmt sequence 1;
Break;
Case const2: stmt sequence 2;
Break;
:
:
Case const n-1: stmt sequence n-1;
Break;
Default: stmt seq n;
}

Example:-
Int main()
{
Int dow;
Cin>>dow;
Switch(dow)
{
Case 1: cout<<"Sunday";
Break;
Case 2: cout<<"Monday";
Break;
Case 3: cout<<"Tuesday";
Break;
:
:
Case 7: cout<<"Saturday";
Break;
Default: cout<<"no entry";
}
Return 0;

Loops and iteration:-

The iteration statements allow a set of instructions to be performed repeatedly until a certain condition occurs or fulfilled. Iteration is also called loops.

- The for loop
- The while loop
- The do-while loop

The for loop:-

> Syntax:-
> For (initialization exp; test-exp;increment exp)
> Body of the loop
> Example:-
> Int main()
> {
> Int I;
> For(i=1;i<=10;i++)
> Cout<<"\n"<<I;
> Return 0;
> }

For loop variations:-

❖   Multiple initialization and update

For(i=1;sum=0;i<=n;sum+=I;++i)
Cout<<I;

❖   Prefer prefix increment/decrement operator over prefix:-

For(i=1;i<n;++i)
Rather than
For(i=1;i<n;i++)

❖   Optional expressions

> In for loop, initialization expression,test expression and update expression are optional.
> For(;test-exp;update-exp)

❖   Infinite loop

> Examples for(j=25; ;--i)
> For(; ;)

❖   Empty loop:- does not contain any statements in loop body

For(j=20;(j);--j)

While loop:- entry controlled loop. While loop can have infinite loop or empty loop.

> Syntax:- while(expression)
> Loop body
> Example:- int main()
> {
> Unsigned long I, num, fact=1;
> Cin>>num;
> While(num)
> {
> Fact=fact*num;
> --num;
> }
> Cout<<fact;
> Return 0;
> }

Do-while loop:- exit controlled loop. It would be executed atleast once even if condition is false.

> Syntax:-
> Do
> {
> Statement;
> }
> While(test-expression);
>
> Example:-
> Char ch='A';
> Do
> {
> Cout<<"\n"<<ch;
> Ch++;
> }
> While(ch<='z');

Nested loops:-

> Example:-
> For(i=1;i<=5;++i)

```
{
Cout<<"\n";
For(j=1;j<=I;++j)
Cout<<"*";
}
```

Jump statements:-unconditionally transfer program control within a function.

Goto statement:- can transfer the program counter anywhere in the program.

> Syntax:-
> Goto label;
> :
> :
> Label:
> Example:-
> A=0;
> Start:
> Cout<<"\n"<<++a;
> If(a<50)
> Goto start;

Break statement:- it enables a program to skip over part of the code. A break statement terminates the smallest enclosing while, do-while, for 0r switch statement;

> Example:-
> While(test exp)
> {
> Stmt 1;
> If(val>2000)
> Break;
> :
> Stmt 2;
> }
> Stmt 3;

Continue statement:-Like break, instead of force termination, it forces the next iteration of loop to take place,skipping any code in between.

> Syntax:-
> While(exp)
> {
> Stmt 1;

```
If(cond)
Continue;
Stmt 2;
}
Stmt 3;
```

Example:-

```
Int a,b,c,I;
For(i=0;i<20;++i)
{
Cout<<"\n enter 2 no. ";
Cin>>a>>b;
If(b==0)
{
Cout<<"enter again";
Continue;
}
Else
C=a/b;
Cout<<c;
}
```

Exit() function:-

Like the break causes the program to terminate as soon as it is encountered.

Example:-

```
If(num%i==0)
{
Cout<<"not a prime number.";
Exit(0);
}
```

➢ Write a program whether the given number is palindrome or not

```
Int main()
{
Int n,num,digit,rev=0;
Cout<<"input the number";
Cin>>num;
N=num;
```

```
Do
{
Digit=num%10;
Rev=(rev*10)+digit;
Num=num/10;
}while(num!=0)
Cout<<"the reverse of the number is:"<<rev;
If(n==rev)
Cout<<"no. is palindrome";
Else
Cout<<"not a palindrome";
Return 0;
}
```

➢   Write a program to print first n natural nymbers and their sum.

```
Int main()
{
Int I,sum,n;
Cout<<"how many natural no's";
Cin>>n;
For(i=1;sum=0;i<=n;i++)
{
Cout<<"\n"<<I;
Sum=sum+I;
}
Cout<<"\n"<<"the    sum    of    first"<<n<<"natural    no.
is:"<<sum<<"\n";
Return 0;
}
```

➢   Write a program to find whether a number is prime or not.

```
Int main()
{
Int num,I;
If(num==1)
Cout<<"prime\n";
Else
{
For(i=2;i<num;++i)
If(num%i==0)
```

```
{
Cout<<"not prime \n";
Exit(0);
}
Cout<<"prime \n";
}
Return 0;
}
```

MCQ's of Control Structures

Question 1: Find out the error in following block of code.

If (x = 100)

Cout << "x is 100";

a.   100 should be enclosed in quotations
b.   There is no semicolon at the end of first line
c.   Equals to operator mistake
d.   Variable x should not be inside quotation

Question 2: Looping in a program means

a.   Jumping to the specified branch of program
b.   Repeat the specified lines of code
c.   Both of above
d.   None of above

Question 3: The difference between while structure and do structure for looping is

a.   In while statement the condition is tested at the end of first iteration

b.   In do structure the condition is tested at the beginning of first iteration

c.   The do structure decides whether to start the loop code or not whereas while statement   decides whether to repeat the code or not

d.   In while structure condition is tested before executing statements inside loop whereas in do structure condition is tested before repeating the statements inside loop

Question 4: Which of the following is not a looping statement in C?

a.   while
b.   until
c.   do
d.   for

Question 5: Which of the following is not a jump statement in C++?

a.   break
b.   goto
c.   exit
d.   switch

Question 6: Which of the following is selection statement in C++?

a.   break

b.   goto

c.   exit

d.   switch

Question 7: The continue statement

a.   resumes the program if it is hanged

b.   resumes the program if it was break was applied

c.   skips the rest of the loop in current iteration

d.   all of above

Question 8: Consider the following two pieces of codes and choose the best answer

CODE 1:

```
switch (x) {
case  1:
         cout <<"x is 1";
         break;
         case 2:
                  cout <<"x is 2";
                  break;
default:
                  cout <<"value of x unknown";
         }


         CODE 2
         If (x==1){
                  Cout <<"x is 1";
                  }
         Else if (x==2){
                  Cout << "x is 2";
                  }
         Else{
                  Cout <<"value of x unknown";
         }
```

a. Both of the above code fragments have the same behaviour

b. Both of the above code fragments produce different effects

c. The first code produces more results than second

d. The second code produces more results than first.

Question 9: Observe the following block of code and determine what happens when x=2?

switch (x){

case 1:

case 2:

case 3:

cout<< "x is 3, so jumping to third branch";

goto thirdBranch;

default:

cout<<"x is not within the range, so need to say Thank You!";

}

a. Program jumps to the end of switch statement since there is nothing to do for x=2

b. The code inside default will run since there is no task for x=2, so, default task is run

c. Will display x is 3, so jumping to third branch and jumps to thirdBranch.

d. None of above

Question 10: Which of the following is false for switch statement in C++?

a. It uses labels instead of blocks

b. we need to put break statement at the end of the group of statement of a condition

c. we can put range for case such as case 1..3

d. None of above

Question 11: How many sequence of statements are present in C++?

a. 4

b. 3

c. 5

d.   6

Question 12: The if..else statement can be replaced by which operator?

a.   Bitwise operator

b.   Conditional operator

c.   Multiplicative operator

d.   none of the mentioned

Question 13: The switch statement is also called as?

a.   choosing structure

b.   selective structure

c.   certain structure

d.   none of the mentioned

Question 14: The destination statement for the goto label is identified by what label?

a. $

b.   @

c.   *

d.   :

Question 15: What is the output of this program?

```
1.        #include <iostream>
2.        using namespace std;
3.        int main ()
4.        {
5.           int n;
6.           for (n = 5; n > 0; n--)
7.           {
8.              cout << n;
9.              if (n == 3)
10.                break;
11.           }
12.           return 0;
13.        }
```

a.   543

b.   54

c.   5432
d.   53

Question 16: What is the output of this program?

```
#include <iostream>
using namespace std;
int main()
{
    int a = 10;
    if (a < 15)
    {
        time:
        cout << a;
        goto time;
    }
    break;
    return 0;
}
```

a.   1010
b.   10
c.   infinitely print 10
d.   compile time error

Question 17: What is the output of this program?

```
#include <iostream>
using namespace std;
int main()
{
    int n = 15;
    for ( ; ;)
    cout << n;
    return 0;
}
```

a.   error
b.   15
c.   infinite times of printing n
d.   none of the mentioned

Question 18: What is the output of this program?

```
#include <iostream>
using namespace std;
int main()
{
    int i;
    for (i = 0; i < 10; i++);
    {
        cout << i;
    }
    return 0;
}
```

a.   0123456789
b.   10
c.   012345678910
d.   compile time error

Question 19: How many types of loops are there?

a.   4
b.   2
c.   3
d.   1

Question 20:   Which looping process is best used when the number of iterations is known?

a.   For
b.   While
c.   do-while
d.   all looping processes require that the iterations be known

Answers

1.   c.
2.   b.
3.   d.
4.   b.
5.   d.
6.   d.
7.   c.
8.   a.
9.   c.
10.   c.
11.   c.
12.   b.
13   b

14   d
15.   a
16   d
17.   c
18.   b
19   a
20   a

Chapter-5 : Functions

Definition:

A function is a sub-program that acts on data and often returns a value.

A function is a group of statements that together perform a task. Every C++ program has at least one function, which is main (), and all the most trivial programs can define additional functions. You can divide up your code into separate functions.

Advantages of using functions:

Following are the some advantages of functions:

- It makes program handling easier.

- It avoids ambiguity as a small part of the program is dealt with at a time.

- It reduces a program size.

- It makes program more readable and understandable to a programmer.

- You can divide your program in logical blocks. It will make your code clear and easy to understand.

- Use of function avoids typing same pieces of code multiple times. You can call a function to execute same lines of code multiple times without re-writing it.

- Individual functions can be easily tested.

- In case of any modification in the code you can modify only the function without changing the structure of the program.

Structure of a function:

Defining a Function:

The general form of a C++ function definition is as follows:

return_type function_name(parameter list)

{

   body of the function;

}

A C++ function definition consists of a function header and a function body. Here are all the parts of a function:

- **Return Type**: A function may return a value. The return_type is the data type of the value the function returns. Some functions perform the desired operations without returning a value. In this case, the return_type is the keyword void.

- **Function Name:** This is the actual name of the function. The function name and the parameter list together constitute the function signature.

- **Parameters:** A parameter is like a placeholder. When a function is invoked, you pass a value to the parameter. This value is referred to as actual parameter or argument. The parameter list refers to the type, order, and number of the parameters of a function. Parameters are optional; that is, a function may contain no parameters.

- **Function Body:** The function body contains a collection of statements that define what the function does.

Function Declarations

A function declaration tells the compiler about a function name and how to call the function. The actual body of the function can be defined separately.

A function declaration has the following parts:

return_type function_name(parameter list);

Parameter names are not important in function declaration only their type is required, so following is also valid declaration:

int max(int, int);

Function declaration is required when you define a function in one source file and you call that function in another file. In such case, you should declare the function at the top of the file calling the function.

Calling a Function

A function is called or invoked or executed by providing the function name, followed by the parameters being sent enclosed in parenthesis.

A function calling has the following parts:

function_name(parameter list);

Example: Write a Program to print cube of a given number using function.

```
#include<iostream.h>
#include<conio.h>
int main()
{
float cube(float);  //function declaration
float x,y;
cout<<"enter a no.: ";
cin>>x;
y=cube(x);  //function calling and assigning its return value to variable y
cout<<"the cube of "<<x<<" is "<<y;
getch();
return 0;
}
float cube(float a)  //function definition
{
float n;
n=a*a*a;
return(n);
}
```

Return statement

The return statement stops execution and returns to the calling function. When a return statement is executed, the function is terminated immediately at that point, regardless of whether it's in the middle of a loop, etc.

You may have noticed that the return type of main is int, but most examples in this and earlier chapters did not actually return any value from main.

Well, there is a catch: If the execution of main ends normally without encountering a return statement the compiler assumes the function ends with an implicit return statement:

return 0;

Note that this only applies to function main for historical reasons. All other functions with a return type shall end with a proper return statement that includes a return value, even if this is never used.

When main returns zero (either implicitly or explicitly), it is interpreted by the environment as that the program ended successfully.

Because the implicit return 0; statement for main is a tricky exception, some authors consider it good practice to explicitly write the statement.

Formal Arguments and Actual Arguments:

Actual parameters: The parameter that appears in the function call statement are known as actual parameters. At the time of the call each actual parameter is assigned to the corresponding formal parameter in the function definition.

Formal parameters: The parameter that appears in the function definition are known as the formal parameters. Formal parameters are local variables which are assigned values from the arguments when the function is called.

Example:

```
#include<iostream.h>
#include<conio.h>
int main()
{
float cube(float);
float x,y;
cout<<"enter a no.: ";
cin>>x;
y=cube(x); //actual parameters
cout<<"the cube of "<<x<<" is "<<y;
getch();
return 0;
}
float cube(float a)  //formal parameters
 {
float n;
n=a*a*a;
return(n);
}
```

Constant Argument and Default Arguments:

Default Argument: Default arguments are specified at the time of function declaration and are useful when arguments does not passed in function call statement.

Example: float interest (float p, int t, float r=0.10)

   si= interest (5400, 2); //third argument is missing

Constant Argument: Constant arguments are declared using the keyword const. A function cannot modify constant arguments.

Example: length ("a string")

        int sum(const int a, const int b);

Concept of Reference Variable

References allow you to pass parameters to functions by references. When we pass argument by reference, the formal arguments in the called function become aliases to the actual argument in calling function. It means that when the function is working with own arguments, it is actually working on the original data.

Basic Syntax: Declaring a variable as a reference rather than a normal variable simply entails appending an ampersand (&) to the type name, such as this "reference to an int"

int x;

int& foo = x; // foo is now a reference to x so this sets x to 56

foo = 56;

Call By Value:

This method copies the value of actual parameters to formal parameters that is the function creates its own copy of the argument values and then uses them.

Example: WAP to swap two numbers.
```
#include<iostream.h>
#include<conio.h>
int main()
{
void swap(int,int);
int x=7,y=9;
cout<<"original values: ";
cout<<"x="<<x<<"y="<<y;
swap(x,y);
cout<<"after swap: "<<"x= "<<x<<" and "<<"y="<<y;
getch();
return 0;
}
void swap(int a,int b)
{
int temp;
temp=a;
```

```
a=b;
b=temp;
cout<<"swapped values:"<<"x="<<x<<"y="<<y;
}
```

Call By Reference:

Instead of passing a value to the function being called, a reference to the original variable is passed. Reference is an alias for predefined variable.

Example: WAP to swap two numbers.

```
#include<iostream.h>
#include<conio.h>
int main()
{
void swap(int &, int &);
int x=7,y=9;
cout<<"original values: ";
cout<<"x="<<x<<"y="<<y;
swap(x,y);
cout<<"after swap: "<<"x=  "<<x<<" and "<<"y="<<y;
getch();
return 0;
}
void swap(int &a, int &b)
{
int temp;
temp=a;
a=b;
b=temp;
cout<<"swapped values:"<<"x="<<x<<"y="<<y;
}
```

Library Functions:

The C++ Standard Library provides a rich collection of functions for performing common mathematical calculations, string manipulations, character manipulations, input/output, error checking and many other useful operations. This makes the programmer's job easier, because these functions provide many of the capabilities programmers need. The C++ Standard Library functions are provided as part of the C++ programming environment.

Math library function: it is used for certain commonly used calculations.

Function	Purpose
sin(x)	To find trigonometric sine of x
Cos(x)	To find trigonometric cosine of x
sqrt(x)	To find square root of x
exp(x)	To find exponential of x
log(x)	To find natural logarithm of x (base e)
pow(x,y)	To find x raised to power y.
tan(x)	To find trigonometric tangent of x

Recursion:

If a program allows you to call a function inside the same function, then it is called a recursive call of the function. In other words calling of function itself again and again.

Example: WAP to swap two numbers.

```
#include<iostream.h>
#include<conio.h>
int main()
{
long int fact(long int);
long int f,n;
cout<<"enter value: ";
cin>>n;
f=fact(n);
cout<<"factorial is: "<<f;
getch();
return 0;
}
long int fact(long int n)
{
long int fact(long int);
long int value=1;
if(n==1)
return(value);
else
value=n*fact(n-1);
}
```

Storage Classes:

Storage class of a variable defines the lifetime and visibility of a variable. Lifetime means the duration till which the variable remains active and visibility defines in which module of the program the variable is accessible. There are five types of storage classes in C++. They are:

1. Automatic
2. External
3. Static
4. Register
5. Mutable

Storage Class	Keyword	Lifetime	Visibility	Initial Value
Automatic	auto	Function Block	Local	Garbage
External	extern	Whole Program	Global	Zero
Static	static	Whole Program	Local	Zero
Register	register	Function Block	Local	Garbage
Mutable	mutable	Class	Local	Garbage

1. Automatic Storage Class

Automatic storage class assigns a variable to its default storage type. *auto* keyword is used to declare automatic variables. However, if a variable is declared without any keyword inside a function, it is automatic by default. This variable is **visible** only within the function it is declared and its **lifetime** is same as the lifetime of the function as well. Once the execution of function is finished, the variable is destroyed.

Syntax of Automatic Storage Class Declaration
datatype var_name1 [= value];
or
auto datatype var_name1 [= value];

2. External Storage Class

External storage class assigns variable a reference to a global variable declared outside the given program. *extern* keyword is used to declare external variables. They are **visible** throughout the program and its **lifetime** is same as the lifetime of the program where it is declared. This visible to all the functions present in the program.

Syntax of External Storage Class Declaration
extern datatype var_name1;

3. Static Storage Class

Static storage class ensures a variable has the **visibility** mode of a local variable but **lifetime** of an external variable. It can be used only within the function where it is declared but destroyed only after the program execution has finished. When a function is called, the variable defined as static inside the function retains its previous value and operates on it. This is mostly used to save values in a recursive function.

Syntax of Static Storage Class Declaration
static datatype var_name1 [= value];

4. Register Storage Class

Register storage assigns a variable's storage in the CPU registers rather than primary memory. It has its lifetime and visibility same as automatic variable. The purpose of creating register variable is to increase access speed and makes program run faster. If there is no space available in register, these variables are stored in main memory and act similar to variables of automatic storage class. So only those variables which requires fast access should be made register.

Syntax of Register Storage Class Declaration
register datatype var_name1 [= value];

5. Mutable Storage Class

In C++, a class object can be kept constant using keyword *const*. This doesn't allow the data members of the class object to be modified during program execution. But, there are cases when some data members of this constant object must be changed.

For example, during a bank transfer, a money transaction has to be locked such that no information could be changed but even then, its state has be changed from - *started* to *processing* to *completed*. In those cases, we can make these variables modifiable using a **mutable** storage class.

Syntax for Mutable Storage Class Declaration

mutable datatype var_name1;

MCQ's of Functions

1.   Which of the following function prototype is perfectly acceptable?
A.   int Function(int Tmp = Show());
B.   float Function(int Tmp = Show(int, float));
C.   Both A and B.
D.   float = Show(int, float) Function(Tmp);

2.   Which of the following statement is correct?
A.   C++ enables to define functions that take constants as an argument.
B.   We cannot change the argument of the function that that are declared as constant.
C.   Both A and B.
D.   We cannot use the constant while defining the function.

3.   Which of the following statement is correct?
A.   Overloaded functions can have at most one default argument.
B.   An overloaded function cannot have default argument.
C.   All arguments of an overloaded function can be default.
D.   A function if overloaded more than once cannot have default argument.

4.   Which of the following statement is correct?
A.   Two functions having same number of argument, order and type of argument can be overloaded if both functions do not have any default argument.
B.   Overloaded function must have default arguments.
C.   Overloaded function must have default arguments starting from the left of argument list.
D.   A function can be overloaded more than once.

5.   Which of the following statement will be correct if the function has three arguments passed to it?
A.   The trailing argument will be the default argument.
B.   The first argument will be the default argument.
C.   The middle argument will be the default argument.
D.   All the argument will be the default argument.

6.   Which of the following statement is incorrect?
A.   Default arguments can be provided for pointers to functions.
B.   A function can have all its arguments as default.
C.   Default argument cannot be provided for pointers to functions.
D.   A default argument cannot be redefined in later declaration.

7.   Which of the following statement is correct?
A.   Constructors can have default parameters.
B.   Constructors cannot have default parameters.
C.   Constructors cannot have more than one default parameter.
D.   Constructors can have at most five default parameters.

8.   Which of the following function / type of function cannot be overloaded?
A.   Member function
B.   Static function
C.   Virtual function
D.   Both B and C

9.   Which of the following function declaration is/are incorrect?
A.   int Sum(int a, int b = 2, int c = 3);
B.   int Sum(int a = 5, int b);
C.   int Sum(int a = 0, int b, int c = 3);
D.   Both B and C are incorrect.
E.   All are correct.

10. Which of the following statement is incorrect?
A.   The default value for an argument can be a global constant.
B.   The default arguments are given in the function prototype.
C.   Compiler uses the prototype information to build a call, not the function definition.
D.   The default arguments are given in the function prototype and should be repeated in the function definition.

11. Where the default value of parameter have to be specified?
A.   Function call
B.   Function definition
C.   Function prototype
D.   Both B or C

12. Which of the following statement is correct?
A.   The default value for an argument cannot be function call.
B.   C++ allows the redefinition of a default parameter.
C.   Both A and B.
D.   C++ does not allow the redefinition of a default parameter.

13. Which of the following statement is correct?
A.   Only one parameter of a function can be a default parameter.
B.   Minimum one parameter of a function must be a default parameter.
C.   All the parameters of a function can be default parameters.
D.   No parameter of a function can be default.

14. Which of the following statement is incorrect?
A.   A default argument is checked for type at the time of declaration and evaluated at the time of call.
B.   We can provide a default value to a particular argument in the middle of an argument list.
C.   We cannot provide a default value to a particular argument in the middle of an argument list.
D.   Default arguments are useful in situations where some arguments always have the same value.

15. Which of the following statement is correct?
A. Overloaded functions can accept same number of arguments.
B. Overloaded functions always return value of same data type.
C. Overloaded functions can accept only same number and same type of arguments.
D. Overloaded functions can accept only different number and different type of arguments.

16. Which of the following function / types of function cannot have default parameters?
A. Member function of class
B. main()
C. Member function of structure
D. Both B and C

17. Which of the following statement is correct?
A. The order of the default argument will be right to left.
B. The order of the default argument will be left to right.
C. The order of the default argument will be alternate.
D. The order of the default argument will be random.

18. A function that calls itself for its processing is known as
A. Inline Function
B. Nested Function
C. Overloaded Function
D. Recursive Function

19. Variables inside parenthesis of functions declarations have _____ level access.
A. Local
B. Global
C. Module
D. Universal

20. We declare a function with _____ if it does not have any return type
A. long
B. double
C. void
D. int

   ANSWERS

   1.   Option A

   2.   Option C

   3.   Option C

   4.   Option D

   5.   Option A

6. Option C
7. Option A
8. Option C
9. Option D
10. Option D
11. Option C
12. Option D
13. Option C
14. Option B
15. Option A
16. Option B
17. Option A
18. Option D
19. Option A
20. Option C

Chapter-6 : Arrays and Strings

Array: - Array is a collection of variables of the same type that are referenced by a common are. An array is a series of elements of the same type placed in contiguous memory locations that can be individually referenced by adding an index to a unique identifier.

Types of Arrays:-

  i. **One Dimensional Array**: - Comprised of finite homogeneous elements.

  ii. **Multi-Dimensional Array**: -Comprised of elements, each of which is itself an array. Multidimensional arrays can be described as "arrays of arrays".

Single Dimensional Array:-

Array Declaration Syntax: -

> Type array_name [size];

* Type means base type of an array.

* array_name means the name with which the array will be referenced.

* size means number of an elements the array will hold.

Example: int marks [50];

Program to read marks of 50 students & store them under an array.
```
#include<iostream.h>
#include<conio.h>
int main()
{
Const int size =50;
Float marks[size];
for(int i=0;i<size;i++)
{
cout<<"enter marks of student"<<i+1<<"\n";
cin>>marks[i];
}
cout<<"\n";
for(i=0;i<size;i++)
```

```
cout<<"marks["<<i<<"]
return  0;
}
```

```
Enter marks of student 1
89
Enter marks of student 2
98
Enter marks of student 3
88
Marks[0] =89
Marks[1] =98
Marks[2] =88
```

Program to search for a specific element in a 1-D array (LINEAR SEARCH)

```
#include<iostream.h>
#include<conio.h>
int main()
{
int  A[20], size,I,flag=0,num,pos;
cout<<"\n Enter the no. of elements in the array:";
cin>>size;
cout<<"enter the element of array:";
for (i=0;i<size;i++)
cin>>A[i];
cout<<"\n Enter the elements to be searched for :";
cin>>num;
for(i=0;i<size;i++)
if (A[i]==num)
{
Flag=1;
Pos=I;
Break;
```

Two Dimensional (2-D) Array

A 2D array is an array in which each of array is itself an array for instance. An array A[n]

is an M by N table with M rows and N columns

Containing M*N elements.

Array Declaration Syntax: -

Type array-name[rows][coloumns];

Example: int sales[5][12];

Processing 2D Arrays
```
 int A[2][3]l
int i,j;
for(i=0;i<2;i++)
{
for(j=0;j<3;j++)
{
Cout<<"enter element";
Cin>>A[i][j];
}
}
```

Array of strings:

An array of strings is a 2D character array. The size of first index (rows ,determines the no of strings and the size of second index (columns) determine maximum length of each string.

 Char strings [10][51];

Array initialization:

Type array name[size1]..[size n]={value_list}

Int days_of_month[12]={31,28,31,30,31,30,31,30,31,30,31}

If(flag==0)

Cout<<"\nElement not found";

Else

Cout<<"\n Element found at position"<<pos;

Return 0;

}

Enter the no of elements in the array:5

Enter the elements of array:

1 4 7 9 18

Enter the elements to be searched for :9

Elements found at position 4

String as an Array:

A string is defined as a character array that is terminated by a null character '\0'

Char str[11];

Program to check of a string is palindrome or not

```
    int main()
    {
 char string[80],c;
Cout<<"enter string: ":
Cin.getLine(string,80):
For(int len=0;string[len]!='\0'len++):
Int I,j,flag=1;
For(i=0;j=len-1;i<len/2;i++,j--)
{
If(string[i]!=string[j])
{
flag=0;
Break;
}
}}
If (flag)
Cout<<"it is an palindrome-\n";
Else
Cout<<"it is not a palindrome":
}
Return 0;
```

Calling functions with arrays:

When an array is used as an argument to a function only the address of the array gets passed, not a copy of the entire array. When a function is called with an array name, a pointer to first element in the array is passed into the function.

```
void display(int a[10]); //function prototype
int main()
{
Int age[10],I;
Cout<<"enter elements:\n":
For(i=0;i<10;i++)
Cin>>age[i];
```

```
 display (age);
return 0;
}
Void display(int a[10])
{
for (int i=0;i<10;i++)
Cout<<"\n"<<a[i];
}
```

String:

Strings are objects that represent sequences of characters.

The standard string class provides support for such objects with an interface similar to that of a <u>standard container</u> of bytes, but adding features specifically designed to operate with strings of single-byte characters.

Initialization:

Char ch[3]={'r','a','m'}

    Or

Char ch[3]="ram"

Memory Representation of One dimensional array

     Char grade[8];

grade[0]	grade[1]	grade[2]	grade[3]	grade[4]	grade[5]	grade[6]	grade[7]
2000	2001	2002	2003	2004	2005	2006	2007

     int age[5];

age[0]	age[0]	age[1]	age[1]	age[2]	age[2]	age[3]	age[3]	age[4]	age[4]
	5000		5002		5004		5006		5008

The amount of storage required to hold an array is directly related to its type & size

Total bytes = size of(type)*size_of_array.

For above e.g

Total bytes=2*5=10 bytes

Memory Representation of Two dimensional Array:

	0	1	....	N-1
0				
1	A[1][0]			
.				
.				
N-1			A[N-1][...]	

Total bytes= number of rows*no of coloums*size of (base type)

     For e.g.

Int pay[5][7];

Total bytes=5*7*2=70 bytes

Input and Output of strings (read and write)

```
void main()
{
Char name[20];
Cout<<"enter the name";
Cin>>name;
Cout<<"name is"<<name;
}
```

String manipulation function:

String Concatenation strcat():

The strcat() function is used to join two strings . This function appends the contents of source string at the end of the target string.

Syntax: Strcat(string1,string2);

```
Void main()
{
Char s1="hello";
Char s2="bye";
Strcat(s1,s2);
Cout<<"name";
Cout<<s1;
Cout<<"name";
Cout<<s2;
```

o/p :- name

hellobye

name

bye

String Compare strcmp():

The strcmp() function is used to compare two strings .

Syntax: strcmp(s1,s2)

```
void main()
{
Int n;
Char s1="RAM";
Char s2="RAM";
N=strcmp(s1,s2);
If(n==0)
Cout<<"both are same";
Else
Cout<<"both are not same";
}
```

String length: strlen()

This function is used to calculate length of string

Syntax:strlen(string)

N= strlen("singh")

N=5

String reverse strrev():

This function is used to reverse a string.

```
Syntax: strrev(string)
Void main()
]{
Char string1[20];
Cout<<"enter string";
Cin>>string1;
Strrev(string1);
Cout<<"reversed string"<<string1;
}
```

Storage class: - The storage class of a variable tells about which part of program can access it and also tells about its existence

In c++, storage classes are of following types:-

1.   **Automatic:** if a variable is defined within a function it is known as automatic variable or local variable. Variable defined inside main() are also automatic because main() is also a function.

A keyword auto is used to specify automatic variable and it is optional.

General syntax is:

auto data type variable1,variable2.........;

for ex-

auto int a,b;

2.   **External/Global**: It is defined outside of any function i.e the variable which is defined in between header files of program and main() function.
Eg-
#include<iostream.h>
Int a,b;   //external variable
Float c,d   //external variable
Void main()
{

           _____

           _____

}
Extern is the keyword used to declare them and it is also an optional.
E.g. extern int a,b;

3.   **Static:** It is same as a local variable but the only difference is that there are initialized only one of the beginning. Value is same for any function in program.

4.   **Register:** all the variables are stored in memory. As accessing a memory location takes time more than accessing one of the machine register, therefore we can store a variable in register with the help of register storage class

Syntax: register data type n1, n2.......

WAP to differentiate b/w local and global variable

```
#include<iostream.h>
#include<conio.h>
Int x=20;      //external variable
Void main()
{
Int x=10;
Cout<<"local x is:"<<x<<endl;
Cout<<"global x is:"<<::x;
```

Scope resolution operator (::) is used to differentiate global variable

Output:

local x is: 10

global x is: 20

Multiple Choice Questions

1. Which of the following correctly declares an array?
A. int anarray[10];
B. int anarray;
C. anarray{10};
D. array anarray[10];

2. What is the index number of the last element of an array with 29 elements?
A. 29
B. 28
C. 0
D. Programmer-defined

3. Which of the following is a two-dimensional array?
A. array anarray[20][20];
B. int anarray[20][20];
C. int array[20, 20];
D. char array[20];

4. Which of the following correctly accesses the seventh element stored in foo, an array with 100 elements?
A. foo[6];
B. foo[7];
C. foo(7);
D. foo;

5. Which of the following gives the memory address of the first element in array foo, an array with 100 elements?
A. foo[0];
B. foo;
C. &foo;
D. foo[1];

6. Which of the following correctly declares an array?
a) int array[10];
b) int array;
c) array{10};
d) array array[10];

7. What is the index number of the last element of an array with 9 elements?
a) 9
b) 8

c) 0

d) Programmer-defined

8. What is a array?

a) An array is a series of elements of the same type in contiguous memory locations

b) An array is a series of element

c) An array is a series of elements of the same type placed in non-contiguous memory locations

d) None of the mentioned

9. Which of the following accesses the seventh element stored in array?

a) array[6];

b) array[7];

c) array(7);

d) array;

10. Which of the following gives the memory address of the first element in array?

a) array[0];

b) array[1];

c) array(2);

d) array;

11. What will be the output of this program?

```
1.      #include <stdio.h>
2.      using namespace std;
3.      int array1[] = {1200, 200, 2300, 1230, 1543};
4.      int array2[] = {12, 14, 16, 18, 20};
5.      int temp, result = 0;
6.      int main()
7.      {
8.          for (temp = 0; temp < 5; temp++) {
9.              result += array1[temp];
10.         }
11.         for (temp = 0; temp < 4; temp++) {
12.             result += array2[temp];
13.         }
14.         cout << result;
15.         return 0;
16.     }
```

a)6553

b) 6533

c) 6522

d) 12200

12. What will be the output of the this program?

```
1.      #include <stdio.h>
2.      using namespace std;
3.      int main ()
4.      {
```

```
5.          int array[] = {0, 2, 4, 6, 7, 5, 3};
6.          int n, result = 0;
7.          for (n = 0; n < 8; n++) {
8.              result += array[n];
9.          }
10.         cout << result;
11.         return 0;
12.     }
```

a) 25

b) 26

c) 27

d) None of the mentioned

13. What is the output of this program?

```
1.      #include <stdio.h>
2.      using namespace std;
3.      int main()
4.      {
5.          int a = 5, b = 10, c = 15;
6.          int arr[3] = {&a, &b, &c};
7.          cout << *arr[*arr[1] - 8];
8.          return 0;
9.      }
```

a) 15

b) 18

c) garbage value

d) compile time error

14. What is the output of this program?

```
1.      #include <stdio.h>
2.      using namespace std;
3.      int main()
4.      {
5.          char str[5] = "ABC";
6.          cout << str[3];
7.          cout << str;
8.          return 0;
9.      }
```

a) ABC

b) ABCD

c) AB

d) None of the mentioned

15 What is the output of this program?

```
1.      #include <stdio.h>
2.      using namespace std;
3.      int main()
4.      {
5.          int array[] = {10, 20, 30};
6.          cout << -2[array];
7.          return 0;
8.      }
```

a) -15

b) -30

c) compile time error

d) garbage value

16. How many types of representation are in string?

a) 1

b) 2

c) 3

d) 4

17. What is the header file for the string class?

a) #include<ios>

b) #include<str>

c) #include<string>

d) None of the mentioned

18. Which is used to return the number of characters in the string?

a) length

b) size

c) both a & b

d) None of the mentioned

19. What is the output of this program?

```
1.      #include <iostream>
2.      #include <string>
3.      using namespace std;
4.      int main ()
5.      {
6.          string str ("microsoft");
7.          string::reverse_iterator r;
8.          for (r = str.rbegin() ; r < str.rend(); r++ )
9.              cout << *r;
10.         return 0;
11.     }
```

a) microsoft

b) micro

c) tfosorcim

d) tfos

20. What is the output of this program?

```
1.      #include <iostream>
2.      #include <string>
3.      using namespace std;
4.      int main ()
5.      {
6.          string str ("Ubuntu");
7.          cout << str.capacity();
8.          cout << str.max_size();
9.          return 0;
10.     }
```

a) 61073741820

b) 51073741820

c) 6 and max size depends on compiler
d) none of the mentioned

Chapter- 7 : Concepts of Object Oriented Programming

Concept of Object Oriented Programming:

Evolution of Software:

There are two types of programming languages:

1. Low Level Language i.e. machine language and assembly language

2. High Level Language i.e. language using keywords, constructor, easier to write programs

Programming Paradigms:

By paradigms we mean a way of thinking or doing thing. It means organizing principle of a program. It is an approach to programming.

There are following paradigms:

1. **Procedural Programming:** A programming in a procedural language is a list of instructions where each statement tells the computer to do something. In this the whole focus is on processing.

2. **Modular Programming:** In this programming is divided into smaller units i.e. functions (sub- programs) and then grouping the number of functions together into a large entity called module. A set of related program with data they manipulate is called a module. It is also known as hiding principle.

It has one disadvantage that since many modules access the same data so the way the data stored becomes critical.

3. **Object Oriented Programming (OOPs):** This approach views a problem in terms of objects involved rather than procedure for doing it. Object is an identifiable identity with some characteristics and behavior.

For Example: Orange is an object. Its characteristics are: spherical shape, orange color, juicy behavior.

In OOPs characteristics are up by data and its behavior by functions. Therefore, in OOPs object represents an entity that has data and has its interface through functions.

Introduction to Classes

The classes are the most important feature of C++ that leads to Object Oriented programming. Class is a user defined data type, which holds its own data members and member functions, which can be accessed and used by creating instance of that class.

The variables inside class definition are called as data members and the functions are called member functions. A class is a template representing a group of objects that shares common properties and relationship.

Objects

Class is mere a blueprint or a template. No storage is assigned when we define a class. Objects are instances of class, which holds the data variables declared in class and the member functions work on these class objects.

Each object has different data variables. Objects are initialized using special class functions called Constructors. We will study about constructors later.

And whenever the object is out of its scope, another special class member function called Destructor is called, to release the memory reserved by the object.

Basic concept of OOPs:

The OOPs includes the following concepts:

1.   Data abstraction
2.   Data encapsulation
3.   Polymorphism
4.   Inheritance

1.   **Data Abstraction:** Data abstraction refers to the act of representing essential features without including the background details or explanations. Data abstraction refers to, providing only essential information to the outside world and hiding their background details, i.e., to represent the needed information in program without presenting the details.

Data abstraction provides two important advantages:

*   Class internals are protected from inadvertent user-level errors, which might corrupt the state of the object.

*   The class implementation may evolve over time in response to changing requirements or bug reports without requiring change in user-level code.

2. **Data Encapsulation:** The wrapping up of data and operations into a single unit is called as encapsulation. The only way to access the data is using the member functions i.e. data cannot be accessed directly.

3. **Polymorphism:** The process of representing one Form in multiple forms is known as **Polymorphism.** Here one form represent original form or original method always resides in base class and multiple forms represents overridden method which resides in derived classes. Polymorphism is derived from two Greek words: **poly** and morphs. The word "poly" means many and **morphs** means forms. So polymorphism means many forms.

Type of polymorphism

*   Compile time polymorphism
*   Run time polymorphism

*   **Compile time polymorphism:** In C++ programming you can achieve compile time polymorphism in two way, which is given below;
    ✓ Method Overloading
    ✓ Method Overriding

    ✓ **Method Overloading**: Whenever same method name is exiting multiple times in the same class with different number of parameter or different order of parameters or different types of parameters is known as **method overloading**.

    ✓ **Method Overriding:** Define any method in both base class and derived class with same name, same parameters or signature, this concept is known as **method overriding.**

*   **Run time polymorphism:** In C++ Run time polymorphism can be achieve by using <u>virtual function</u>.

Virtual Function: A **virtual function** is a member function of class that is declared within a base class and re-defined in derived class.

When you want to use same function name in both the base and derived class, then the function in base class is declared as virtual by using the **virtual** keyword and again re-defined this function in derived class without using virtual keyword.

Syntax:

```
virtual return_type function_name()
        {
        .......
        .......
        }
```

4.   **Inheritance:** Inheritance is the capability of one class to inherit capabilities or properties of another class. The process of obtaining the data members and methods from one class to another class is known as **inheritance**. It is one of the fundamental features of object-oriented programming.

Important points

- In the inheritance the class which is give data members and methods is known as base or super or parent class.

- The class which is taking the data members and methods is known as sub or derived or child class.

Advantage of inheritance

If we develop any application using this concept than that application have following advantages,

- Application development time is less.

- Application takes less memory.

- Application execution time is less.

- Application performance is enhancing (improved).

- Redundancy (repetition) of the code is reduced or minimized so that we get consistence results and less storage cost.

Types of Inheritance

Based on number of ways inheriting the feature of base class into derived class it have five types they are:

- Single inheritance

- Multilevel inheritance

- Hierarchical inheritance

- Multiple inheritance

- Hybrid inheritance

Single inheritance:

In single inheritance there exists single base class and single derived class.

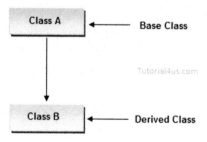

Multilevel inheritances

In multilevel inheritances there exists single base class, single derived class and multiple intermediate base classes.

Intermediate base classes: An intermediate base class is one in one context with access derived class and in another context same class access base class.

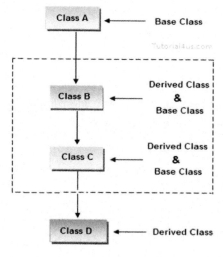

Hence all the above three inheritance types are supported by both classes and interfaces.

Multiple inheritance

In multiple inheritances there exist multiple classes and single derived class.

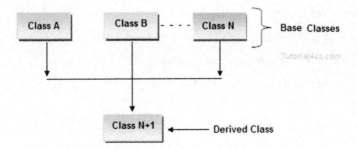

Hierarchical inheritance

When more than one class is derived from a single base class, such inheritance is known as **Hierarchical Inheritance**, where features that are common in lower level are included in parent class.

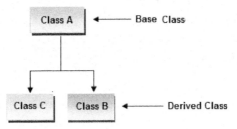

Hybrid inheritance

Combination of any inheritance type

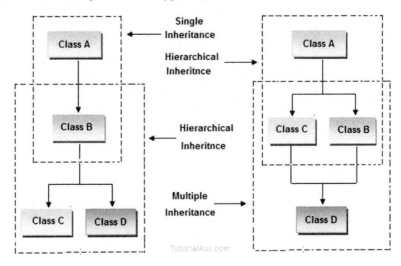

Advantages of OOPs:

• OOP provides a clear modular structure for programs.

• It is good for defining abstract data types.

• Implementation details are hidden from other modules and other modules has a clearly defined interface.

• It is easy to maintain and modify existing code as new objects can be created with small differences to existing ones.

• objects, methods, instance, message passing, inheritance are some important properties provided by these particular languages

• Encapsulation, polymorphism, abstraction are also counts in these fundamentals of programming language.

• It implements real life scenario.

• In OOP, programmer not only defines data types but also deals with operations applied for data structures.

Disadvantages of OOPs:

• Object oriented programs require a lot of work to create. Specifically, a great deal of planning goes into an object oriented program well before a single piece of code is ever written. Initially, this early effort was felt by many to be a waste of time. In addition, because the programs were large coders spent more time actually writing the program.

• Object oriented programs are slower than other programs, partially because of their size. Other aspects of Object Oriented Programs also demand more system resources, thus slowing the program down.

MULTIPLE CHOICE QUESTIONS AND ANSWERS

1.   True/False: A class can serve as base class for many derived classes.
Answer: True

2.   When a class serves as base class for many derived classes, the situation is called:
1.   polymorphism
2.   hierarchical inheritance
3.   hybrid inheritance
4.   multipath inheritance
5.   none of these
Answer: (b)

3.   When two or more classes serve as base class for a derived class, the situation is known as _____.
1.   multiple inheritance
2.   polymorphism
3.   encapsulation
4.   hierarchical inheritance
5.   none of these
Answer: (a)

4.   Multiple inheritance leaves room for a derived class to have _____ members.
1.   dynamic
2.   private
3.   public
4.   ambiguous
5.   none of these
Answer: (d)

5.   Hybrid inheritance is _____.
1.   multiple inheritance
2.   multilevel inheritance
3.   multipath inheritance ...

6.   Reusability is a desirable feature of a language as it
   A. decreases the testing time
   B. lowers the maintenance cost
   C. reduces the compilation time
   D. Both (a) and (b)

7.   Choose the correct remarks.

A. C++ allows any operator to be overloaded.

B. Some of the existing operators cannot be overloaded.

C. Operator precedence cannot be changed.

D. All of the above

8.   C++ was originally developed by;

A. Clocksin and Mellish

B. Donald E. Knuth

C. Sir Richard Hadlee

D. Bjame Stroustru

9 **Dynamic dispatch is a feature that**

- Published on 19 Oct 15

a. selects which polymorphic operation to call at run time

b. selects which polymorphic operation to call at compile time

c. Both a and b

d. None

10 **Break statement in switch case**

- Published on 19 Oct 15

a. prevents from fallthrough

b. causes an exit from innermost loop

c. both a and b

d. none

11 This set of Object Oriented System Design Multiple Choice Questions & Answers (MCQs) focuses on "Object Oriented Programming Principles".

1. Which of the following is the functionality of 'Data Abstraction'?

a) Reduce Complexity

b) Binds together code and data

c) Parallelism

d) None of the mentioned

Answer: a

12 Which of the following mechanisms is/are provided by Object Oriented Language to implement Object Oriented Model?

a) Encapsulation

b) Inheritance

c) Polymorphism

d) All of the mentioned

Answer: d

13 Which of the these is the functionality of 'Encapsulation'?

a) Binds together code and data

b) Using single interface for general class of actions.

c) Reduce Complexity

d) All of the mentioned

Answer: a

14 What is 'Basis of Encapsulation'?

a) object

b) class

c) method

d) all of the mentioned

Answer: d

15. How will a class protect the code inside it?

a) Using Access specifiers

b) Abstraction

c) Use of Inheritance

d) All of the mentioned

Answer: a

16. Which of the following is a mechanism by which object acquires the properties of another object?

a) Encapsulation

b) Abstraction

c) Inheritance

d) Polymorphism

Answer: c

17 Which of the following supports the concept of hierarchical classification?

a) Polymorphism

b) Encapsulation

c) Abstraction

d) Inheritance

Answer: d

18 Which Keyword from the following is used to inherit properties from one class into another?
a) extends
b) subclasses
c) native
d) all of the mentioned
Answer: a

19 Which of the following concept is often expressed by the phrase, 'One interface, multiple methods'?
a) Abstraction
b) Polymorphism
c) Inheritance
d) Encapsulation
Answer: b

20
Which of the following type of class allows only one object of it to be created?
A.Virtual class
B.Abstract class
C.Singleton class
D.Friend class
Answer: Option C

Chapter 8 : Classes and Objects

Class:- A class is a way to bind the data as its associated functions together. It allows data (and functions) to be hidden.

A class specification has two parts:-

1.   Class declaration

2.   Class function definations

The class declaration describes the type and scope of its members. The class function definations describe how the class functions are implemented.

General form of a class declaration:

Class class_name

{

Private:

Variable declaration;

Function declaration;

Public:

Variable declaration;

Function declaration;

};

Functions and variables are collectively called class members. Keywords private and public are known as visibility labels. Private member can be accessed only from within class .Public members can be accessed from outside the class also. By default, all the members are private. So private keywords is optional.

Variable declared inside the class are known as data members and functions are known as member functions.

Example:-

Class item

{

Int number;

Float cost;

Public:

Void getdata (int a, float b);

Void putdata (void);

};

Creating objects:

Once a class has been declared, variables of that type can be created using class name.

Eg.: item x;

Creates a variable x of type item. In C++ ,class variables are known as objects. Moreover one object can be declared in single statement.

Accessing class members:

Object-name.function-name(actual arguments)

x.getdata(100,75.5);

would assign the value 100 to the number and 75.5 to cost.

X.putdata would display the value data members.

Class xyz

{

Int x;

Int y;

Public:

Int z;

};

Xyz=p;

p.x=0;

p.z=10;

Defining member function:-

Member functions can be defined in two places:-

• Outside the class defination.

• Inside the class definition.

<u>Outside</u>:- Member functions that are declared inside a class .A class have to be defined separately outside the class.

<u>General form of a member function is:</u>

Return-type class.name::function name(arg.declaration)

{

Function body

}

The membership label class-name ::tells the computer that the function-name belong to the class-name. The symbol :: is called scope resolution operator.

Void item::getdata (int a, float b)

{

Number=a;

Cost=b;

}

Void item:: putdata(void)

{

Cout<<"number:"<<number<<"\n";

Cout<<"cost:"<<cost<<"\n";

<u>Characteristics of member function:-</u>

- Several different classes can use same function .the membership label will resolve their scope.

- Member function can access the private data in the class. A non-member function cant do so.

- A member function can call another member function directly, without using the dot operator.

<u>Inside the class definition</u>

This method replaces the function declaration the actual function definition inside the class.

Class item

{

Int member;

```
Float cost;
Public:
Void getdata(int a,float b);
Void putdata(void)
{
Cout<<number<<"\n";
Cout<<cost<<"\n";
}
```

A C++ program with class:

```
#include<iostream.h>
Class item
{
Int number;
Float cost;
Public:
Void getdata(int a,float b);
Void putdata(void)
{
Cout<<"number:"<<number<<"\n";
Cout<<"cost:"<<cost<<"\n";
};
Void item:: getdata (int a,float b)
{
Number=a;
Cost=b;
}
Int  main()
{
Item x;
Cout<<"\n object x"<<"\n";
```

x.getdata(100,299.95);

x.putdata();

item y;

cout<<"\n object y"<<"\n";

y.getdata(200,175.50);

y.putdata();

}

Output:

Object x

Number=100

Cost: 299.95

Object y

Number :200

Cost : 175.5

Private member function:

A private member function can be called by aout function that is member of its class.

Class sample

{

Int m;

Void read(void);

Public:

Void update(void);

Void write(void);

};

If s1 is an object of sampke, then

S1.read(); is illegal

However the function read() can be called by the function update() to update the value of m.

Void sample ::update(void)

{

Read();

}

Friend function:

As private members cannot be accessed from outside the class. There may be a situation in which two classes need to show share function. So C++ allow the common function to be made friendly with both the classes. To make an outside function "friendly" to a class.

```
Class abc
{
.........
Public:
.........
Friend void xyz(void);
};
```

Friend function characteristics:

- It is not in the scope of the class to which it has been declared as friend.

- It can't be called using the object of the class.

- It can be invoked like a normal function without the help of any object.

- Unlike member functions, it can't access the member names directly and has to use an object name and dot membership operators with each member name.

- It can be declared either in public or private part.

- Usually it has the objects and arguments.

```
Class sample
{
Int a;
Int b;
Public:
Void setvalue()
{
```

```
A=25;
Friend float mean(sample s);
};
Float mean(sample s)
{
Return float(s.a+s.b)/2.0;
}
Int main()
{
Sample x;
x.setvalue();
cout<<"mean  value="<<mean(x)<<"\n";
return 0;
}
```

Member function of one class can be friend function of another class.

```
Class x
{
……………
……………
};
Class y
{
……………
Friend int x::fun1();
……….
};
```

All member function of one class can be declared as friend function of another class.

```
Class z
{
…………..
Friend class x:
};
```

Constructor:

A constructor is a special member function whose task is to initialize the objects of the class. The constructor is invoked when ever an object of its associated class is called constructor because it constructs the value of data member of the class.

> Eg
>
> Class integer
>
> {
>
> Int m.n;
>
> Public:
>
> Integer(void);
>
> ………….
>
> …………..
>
> };
>
> Integer::integer(void)
>
> {
>
> M=0;n=0;
>
> }
>
> Integer int1;

This willnot only create the object in one of type integer but also initialize its data member m and n to zero.

A constructor that accepts no parameters is called the default constructor.

Characteristics:

- Should be declared in the public section.

- Automatically called when the objects are created.

- Do not have return types.

- Can't be inherited.

- Can have default arguments.

- Can't be virtual.

- Can't refer to their address.

Destructor:

It is used to destroy the object that have been created by the constructor.

~integer()

A destructor never takes any argument nor does it returns any value. It will bw implicitly by the compiler upon exit from the program to clean up storage that is no longer accessible.

Eg:

```
Int count=0;
Class alpha
{
Public:
Alpha()
{
Count ++;
Cout<<"\n no. of objects created "<<count;
}
~alpha()
{
Cout<<"\n no. of objects destroyed"<< count;
Count--;
}
Int main()
{
Cout<<"in main";
Alpha a1 ,a2,a3,a4;
{
Cout<<"\n in block1";
Alpha a3;
}
}
Cout<<"\n in block2";
Alpha a6;
}
Cout<<"\n in main again"
}
```

MCQ on Classes and Objects

Q 1- Which operator is used to resolve the scope of the global variable?

A - -->

B - .

C - *

D - ::

Answer : D

Explaination

Scope resolution operator is used to resolve for the global scope of a variable if the local and global variables conflict by name.

Q.2.

The process of building new classes from existing one is called _____.

(A   Polymorphism

(B) Structure

(C) Inheritance

(D) Cascading

Ans: C

Q.3 Usually a pure virtual function

(A)has complete function body.

(B)will never be called.

(C)will be called only to delete an object.

(D)is defined only in derived class.

Ans: D

Q.4 Overloading the function operator

(A)requires a class with an overloaded operator.

(B)requires a class with an overloaded [ ] operator.

(C)allows you to create objects that act syntactically like functions.

(D)usually make use of a constructor that takes arguments.

Ans: A

Q.5 The keyword friend does not appear in

(A)the class allowing access to another class.

(B)the class desiring access to another class.

(C)the private section of a class.

(D)the public section of a class.
Ans: C

Q.6 A friend function to a class, C cannot access

(A) private data members and member functions.
(B) public data members and member functions.
(C) protected data members and member functions.
(D) the data members of the derived class of C.
Ans: D

Q.7 The operator that cannot be overloaded is

(A) ++
(B)::
(C) ( )
(D) ~
Ans: B

Q.8 Pure virtual functions

(A) have to be redefined in the inherited class.
(B)cannot have publicaccess specification.
(C)are mandatory for a virtual class.
(D)None of the above.
Ans: A

Q.9 Use of virtual functions implies

(A) overloading.
(B)overriding.
(C)static binding.
(D)dynamic binding.
ANS.

Q.10 It is possible to declare as a friend

(A)a member function
(B)a global function
(C)a class
(D)all of the above
Ans:D

Q.11 A virtual class is the same as

(A) an abstract class
(B)a class with a virtual function

(C) a base class

(D)none of the above.

Ans:D

Q.12 In which case is it mandatory to provide a destructor in a class?

(A) Almost in every class

B)Class for which two or more than two objects will be created

(C)Class for which copy constructor is defined

(D)Class whose objects will be created dynamically

Ans:D

Q.13 The members of a class, by default, are

(A) public

(B)protected

(C)private

(D)mandatory to specify

Ans:C

Q.14Given a class named Book,

which of the following is not a valid constructor?

(A) Book ( ) { }

(B) Book (Book b) { }

(C) Book (Book &b) { }

(D)Book (char* author, char* title) { }

Ans:B

Q.15 Which of the following statements is NOT valid about operator overloading?

(A)Only existing operators can be overloaded.

(B)Overloaded operator must have at least one operand

of its class type.

(C)The overloaded operators follow the syntax rules of

the original operator.

(D)none of the above.

Ans:D

Q.16 How many constructors can a class have?

(A)0

(B) 1

(C)2

(D) any number

Ans:D

Q.17 A template class

(A) is designed to be stored in different containers
(B)works with different data types
(C)generates objects which must be identical
(D)generates classes with different numbers of member functions.
Ans:B

Q.18 Which of the following is the valid class declaration header for the derived class with base classes b1and b2?

(A)class d: public b1, public b2
(B)class d: class b1, class b2
(C)class d: public b1, b2
(D)class d: b1, b2
Ans:A

Q.19 A pure virtual function is a virtual function that

(A)has no body
(B) returns nothing
(C)is used in base class
(D) both (A)and (C)
Ans:D

Q.20 A class defined within another class is:

(A) Nested class
(B)Inheritance
(C)Containership
(D) Encapsulation
Ans:A

Chapter 9 : Basics of file handling

A file is a collection of related data stored in a particular area on the disk. Programs can be designed to perform the read and write operations on these files. The input/output system of C++ handles file operations which are very much similar to console input and output operations. It uses file streams as an interface between the programs and the files. The stream that supplies data to the program is known as **input stream** and the one that receives data from the program is known as **output stream** . In other words, input stream extracts (or reads) data from the file and the output stream inserts (or writes) data to the file.

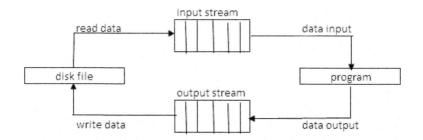

Opening a File:

For opening a file, file stream must be created and then it should be linked to the filename. A file stream can be defined using the classesifstream, ofstream and fstream. A file can be opened in two ways : -

1.   Using the constructor function of the class

2.   Using the member function open ( ) of the class

Opening file using Constructor :

File is used to initialize the file stream object

1.   Create a file stream object to manage the stream using the appropriate class, the class ofstream is used to create the output stream and the class ifstream to create input stream

2.   Initialize the file object with the desired filename.

Ofstream outfile ("results"); // output only , this creates outfile as an ofstream object that manages the output stream.

Ifstream infile ("data"); // input only . It declares infile as an ifstream object and attaches it to the file data for reading (input) .

The connection with a file is closed automatically when the strteam object expires (when the program terminates).

⟶ Both reading and writing can be done in single program like :-

…………………

…………………

Outfile.close ( );

Ifstream infile ("salary");

………………

………………

Infile. Close ( );

Example:--

#include<iostream.h>

#include<fstream.h>

Int main ( )

{

Ofstream outf ("ITEM");   // connect ITEM file to outf

Cout<<"enter item name ";

Char name [30];

Cin>>name;

Outf<<name<<"\n";   // write to file ITEM

Cout<<"enter item cost : ";

float cost;

cin>>cost;

outf<<cost<<"/n";

outf.close( );

ifstream inf("ITEM");   // connect item file to inf

inf>> name ;   // read name from file ITEM

inf >> cost;   // read cost from file ITEM

cout <<"/n";

cout<<"item name :" <<name <<"/n";

cout<< "item cost : "; <<cost <<"/n";

inf.close ( );

return 0 ( );

}

Opening file using open( )

The function open( ) can be used to open multiple files that use same stream object.

File-stream-class   stream – object;

Stream-object.open ("filename");

Example :-

ofstream outfile ;   // create stream (for output)

_outfile.open ("DATA 1 ");   //   connect stream to DATA 1

Outfile.close ( );   // Disconnect stream from DATA 1

Outfile.open ("DATA 2");   // connect stream to DATA 2

Outfile.close ( );   // disconnect stream from DATA 2

Write & read ( ) function :-

It handles data in binary form

The binary input and output functions takes the following form:

Infile.read ((Char*)& V, size of (V));

outfile.write ((Char*)& V, size of (V));

The function's first argument is the address of variable V and second is length of that variable is bytes. The address of the variable must be cast to type char* (i.e pointer to character type)

Example :-

```cpp
#include<iostream.h>
 #include<fstream.h>
#include<iomanip.h>
Const char * filename="BINARY";
Int main( )
{
Float height [4] = { 175.5, 153.0, 167.25, 160.70};
Ofstream outfile;
Outfile.open (filename);
Outfile.write ((char*) & height, size of (height));
Outfile.close( );
For (int i=0; i<4, i++)
Height [i] = 0;
Ifstream.open (filename);
Infile.head ((char*) & height, size of (height ));
For (i=0; i<4; i++)
{
Cout.setf (ios :: showpoint);
Cout<<setn (10 )<< setprecision (2 )<<height[i];
}
Infile.close( )
return 0 ;
}
```

Error handling during File Operations :-

Error handling functions :-

eof ( ) : Returns true (non-zero value) if end –of- file is encountered while reading otherwise return false (zero)

fail ( )   : returns true when an input or output operation has failed.

Bad ( ) : returns true if an invalid operation is attempted or any unrecoverable error has occurred. However , if it is false, it may be possible to recover from any other error reported and continue operation.

Good ( ) : returns true if no error has occurred . This means that all the above functions are false . For instance, if file.good ( )is true, all is well with the stream file and we can proceed to perform input output operations. When it returns false, no further operations can carried out.

Ifstream infile;

Infile.open("ABC");

While (infile.fail( ))

{

Procrss the file

}

If (infile.eof())

--------------------------   // terminate program normally

}

Else

If (infile.bad ( ))

{

------------   (repeat fatal error)

{

else}

{

Infile.clear( );   //clear error
state

}

File handling MCQ

1) By default, all the files are opened in _____mode .
a. Binary
b. Text
c. Can't say

**2) It is not possible to combine two or more file opening mode in open ()
method.**
a. True

b. False

3) Which of the following is not a file opening mode ____ .
a. ios::ate

b. ios::nocreate
c. ios::noreplace
d. ios::truncate

4) Due to ios::trunc mode, the file is truncated to zero lengt
a. True
b. False

**5) If we have object from ofstream class, then default mode of opening the
file is _____ .**

a. ios::in
b. ios::out
c. ios::inios::trunc
d. ios::outios::trunk

6) _____ is return type of is_open() function

a. int
b. bool
c. float
d. char *

**7) If we have object from fstream class, then what is the default mode of
opening the file?**

a. ios::inios::out
b. ios::inios::outios::trunc
c. ios::inios::trunc
d. Default mode depends on compiler

8) To create an output stream, we must declare the stream to be of class _____ .

a. ofstream

b. ifstream

c. iostream

d. None of these

9) Streams that will be performing both input and output operations must be declared as class _____ .

a. iostream

b. fstream

c. stdstream

d. Stdiostream

10) To perform File I/O operations, we must use _____ header file

a. < ifstream>

b. < ofstream>

c. < fstream>

d. Any of these

11) Which of the following is not used to seek a file pointer

a. ios::cur

b. ios::set

c. ios::end

d. ios::beg

12). What is use of eof() ?

a)   Returns true if a file open for reading has reached the next character.

b)   Returns true if a file open for reading has reached the next word.

c)   Returns true if a file open for reading has reached the end.

d)   Returns true if a file open for reading has reached the middle.

13).Which among following is correct syntax of closing a file in c++ ?

a)   myfile$close();

b)   myfile@close();

c)   myfile:close();

d)   myfile.close();

14.) *Which is correct syntax ?*

a)   myfile:open ("example.bin", ios::out);
b)   myfile.open ("example.bin", ios::out);
c)   myfile::open ("example.bin", ios::out);
d)   myfile.open ("example.bin", ios:out);

15.) *What is use of eof() ?*

a)   Returns true if a file open for reading has reached the next character.
b)   Returns true if a file open for reading has reached the next word.
c)   Returns true if a file open for reading has reached the end.
d)   Returns true if a file open for reading has reached the middle.

16.)*Which functions allow to change the location of the get and put positions ?*

a)   sg() and sp()
b)   sekg() and sekp()
c)   gog() and gop()
d)   seekg() and seekp()

17.)*offset counted from the current position using ?*

a)   ios::curr
b)   ios::cr
c)   ios::cur
d)   ios::current

18.)*Calling the stream's member function sync() causes an immediate synchronization.*

a)   True
b)   False

19.)*Which is among following is used to Open a file for output and move the read/write control to the end of the file ?*

a)   ios::ate
b)   ios::at
c)   ios::ann
d)   ios::end

20.)*Which is correct syntax for, position n bytes back from end of fileObject ?*

a)   fileObject.seekg(ios::end, n);
b)   fileObject.seekg(n, ios:end);
c)   fileObject.seekg(n, ios::end);

d)   fileObject.seekg(ios:end,

Answers:-

1-b,2-b,3-d,4-a,5-b,6-b,7-d,8-a,9-c,10-c.11-b,12-c,13-d,14-d, 15-c ,16-d,17-c, 18-a, 19-a, 20-c

University Question Bank

Total No. of Questions : 09

B.Tech.(2011 Onwards) (Sem.-1,2)

FUNDAMENTALS OF COMPUTER PROGRAMMING AND IN FORMATION TECHNOLOGY

Subject Code:BTCS-101   Paper ID : [Al 108]
Time:3Hrs.   Max. Marks:60

INSTRUCTIONS TO CANDIDATES :

1. SECTION-A is COMPULSORY consisting of TEN questions carrying TWO marks each,

2. SECTION - B & C. have FOUR questions each.

3. Attempt any FIVE questions from SECTIONB & C carrying EIGHT marks each.

4. Select at least TWO questions from SECTION

SECTION-A

1.

Write short notes on :

(a)   How two dimensionalarrays are declared and initialized?

The simplest form of multidimensional array is the two-dimensional array. A two-dimensional array is, in essence, a list of one-dimensional arrays. To declare a two-dimensional integer array of size [x][y], you would write something as follows –

typearrayName [x][y];

Where **type** can be any valid C data type and **arrayName** will be a valid C identifier. A two-dimensional array can be considered as a table which will have x number of rows and y number of columns. A two-dimensional array **a**, which contains three rows and four columns can be shown as follows –

	Column 0	Column 1	Column 2	Column 3
Row 0	a[0][0]	a[0][1]	a[0][2]	a[0][3]
Row 1	a[1][0]	a[1][1]	a[1][2]	a[1][3]
Row 2	a[2][0]	a[2][1]	a[2][2]	a[2][3]

Thus, every element in the array **a** is identified by an element name of the form **a[i][j]**, where 'a' is the name of the array, and 'i' and 'j' are the subscripts that uniquely identify each element in 'a'.

Multidimensional arrays may be initialized by specifying bracketed values for each row. Following is an array with 3 rows and each row has 4 columns.

int a[3][4] = {

{0, 1, 2, 3} , /* initializers for row indexed by 0 */

{4, 5, 6, 7} , /* initializers for row indexed by 1 */

{8, 9, 10, 11} /* initializers for row indexed by 2 */

};

The nested braces, which indicate the intended row, are optional. The following initialization is equivalent to the previous example −

int a[3][4] = {0,1,2,3,4,5,6,7,8,9,10,11};

(b) What are the different types of Computer Languages?

Two Basic Types of Computer Language

- **Low-Level Languages:** A language that corresponds directly to a specific machine

- **High-Level Languages:** Any language that is independent of the machine

There are also other types of languages, which include

- **System languages:** These are designed for low-level tasks, like memory and process management

- **Scripting languages:** These tend to be high-level and very powerful

- **Domain-specific languages:** These are only used in very specific contexts

- **Visual languages:** Languages that are not text-based

- **Esoteric languages:** Languages that are jokes or are not intended for serious use

These languages are not mutually exclusive, and some languages can belong to multiple categories. The terms low-level and high-level are also open to interpretation, and some languages that were once considered high-level are now considered low-level as languages have continued to develop.

(c) what is the difference between break andcontinue statement?

The major difference between `break` and `continue` statements in C language is that a `break` causes the innermost enclosing loop or `switch` to be exited immediately. Whereas, the `continue` statement causes the next iteration of the enclosing `for`, `while`, or `do` loop to begin. The `continue` statement in `while` and `do` loops takes the control to the loop's *test-condition* immediately, whereas in the `for` loop it takes the control to the *increment* step of the loop.

The `continue` statement applies only to loops, not to `switch`. A `continue` inside a `switch` inside a loop causes the next loop iteration.

Practically, `break` is used in `switch`, when we want to exit after a particular `case` is executed; and in loops, when it becomes desirable to leave the loop as soon as a certain condition occurs (for instance, you detect an error condition, or you reach the end of your data prematurely).

The `continue` statement is used when we want to skip one or more statements in loop's body and to transfer the control to the next iteration.

(d) What is Access Specifier and its use?

Access specifiers in C++ class defines the access control rules. C++ has 3 new keywords introduced, namely,

1. public

2. private

3. protected

These access specifiers are used to set boundaries for availability of members of class be it data members or member functions

Access specifiers in the program, are followed by a colon. You can use either one, two or all 3 specifiers in the same class to set different boundaries for different class members. They change the boundary for all the declarations that follow them.

(e) Name various control statements of C++.

The if keyword is used to execute a statement or block, if, and only if, a condition is fulfilled. Its syntax is:

if (condition) statement

Here, condition is the expression that is being evaluated. If this condition is true, statement is executed. If it is false, statement is not executed (it is simply ignored), and the program continues right after the entire selection statement. Iteration statements (loops)

Loops repeat a statement a certain number of times, or while a condition is fulfilled. They are introduced by the keywords while, do, and for.

The while loop

The simplest kind of loop is the while-loop. Its syntax is:
while (expression) statement

The do-while loop

A very similar loop is the do-while loop, whose syntax is:
do statement while (condition)

The for loop

The for loop is designed to iterate a number of times. Its syntax is:
for (initialization; condition; increase) statement;

(f) What do you mean by precedence and Associatively.

Precedence of operators

If more than one <u>operators</u> are involved in an expression, C language has a predefined rule of priority for the operators. This rule of priority of operators is called operator precedence.

In C, precedence of arithmetic operators(*, %, /, +, -) is higher than relational operators(==, !=, >, <, >=, <=) and precedence of relational operator is higher than logical operators(&&, || and !).

Example of precedence

(1 > 2 + 3 && 4)

This expression is equivalent to:

((1 > (2 + 3)) && 4)

i.e, (2 + 3) executes first resulting into 5

then, first part of the expression (1 > 5) executes resulting into 0 (false) then, (0 && 4) executes resulting into 0 (false)

(g) Define the term private and protected Inheritance?

protected inheritance

1.   Protected implemented-in-terms-of. Rarely useful. Used in `boost::compressed_pair` to derive from empty classes and save memory using empty base class optimization (example below doesn't use template to keep being at the point):

2.   structempty_pair_impl:protected empty_class_1

3.   { non_empty_class_2 second;};

4.

5.   struct pair :privateempty_pair_impl{

6.   non_empty_class_2 &second(){

7.   returnthis->second;

8.   }

9.

10.   empty_class_1 &first(){

11.   return*this;// notice we return *this!

12.   }

};

private inheritance

1.   Implemented-in-terms-of. The usage of the base class is only for implementing the derived class. Useful with traits and if size matters (empty traits that only contain functions will make use of the empty base class optimization). Often *containment* is the better solution, though. The size for strings is critical, so it's an often seen usage here

2.   template<typenameStorageModel>

3.   struct string :privateStorageModel{

4.   public:

5.   voidrealloc(){

6.   // uses inherited function

7.   StorageModel::realloc();

8.   }

};

(h)Explain the Key features supported by a GUI based operating system.

raphical User Interface (GUI) is a system that allows users to interact with computers. GUI is not an operating system, but rather an interface design on your computer, so computer that you use has a more attractive appearance than the computer a few decades ago.

For many years, GUI technology being developed for the purposes of operating systems like Windows, Macintosh, Linux, Symbian and many more operating systems that require a GUI system to form an attractive display interface. The first operating that use GUI is operating system from Apple, the Macintosh. After a Macintosh, many developers who follow the steps to adopt the GUI system of the Macintosh into their operating system.

Below are some list of GUI-based network operating system and some significant advances in GUI design and appearance of the graphical user interface to the operating systems that exist today. Here's a list of systems that use the base GUI.

i)   Name various standard classes of C++.

A **class** in **C++** is a user defined type or data structure declared with keyword *class* that has data and functions (also called methods) as its members whose access is governed by the three access specifiers *private*, *protected* or *public* (by default access to members of a class is *private*). A class in C++ differs from a structure (declared with keyword *struct*) as by default, members are *private* in a class while they are *public* in a structure. The private members are not accessible outside the class; they can be accessed only through methods of the class. The public members form an interface to the class and are accessible outside the class. Instances of these data types are known as <u>objects</u> and can contain <u>member variables</u>, <u>constants</u>, <u>member functions</u>, and <u>overloaded operators</u> defined by the programmer.

Aggregate classes

An aggregate class is a class with no user-declared constructors, no private or protected non-static data members, no base classes, and no virtual functions.[2] Such a class can be initialized with a brace-enclosed comma-separated list of initializer-clauses.[3] The following code has the same semantics in both C and C++.

j) What is Virtual Memory and its use

Virtual memory is a feature of an operating system (OS) that allows a computer to compensate for shortages of physical memory by temporarily transferring pages of data from random access memory (RAM) to disk storage. Eventually, the OS will need to retrieve the data that was moved to temporarily to disk storage -- but remember, the only reason the OS moved pages of data from RAM to disk storage to begin with was because it was running out of RAM. To solve the problem, the operating system will need to move *other* pages to hard disk so it has room to bring back the pages it needs right away from temporary disk storage. This process is known as *paging* or *swapping* and the temporary storage space on the hard disk is called a pagefile or a swap file.

SECTION-B

2. Discuss in brief the various features provided by any word processor. Also define the terms: Toolbar and Status bar. how can we Activate or deactivate any toolbar?

☐**Wordwrap:** automatic arrangement of text in lines of specified length without the necessity of touching the return key.

☐**Discretionary Hyphenation:** option of inserting a hyphen to break a word that ends a line: the hyphen does not print if later editing moves the word to the middle of a line.

☐**Justification:** automatic alignment of text to both the left and right margins.

☐**Adjustment:** realignment of text to new margin and tab settings.

☐**Alignment:** positioning text or numbers to specified margin and tab settings.

☐**Decimal Alignment:** positioning columns of numbers with the decimal points vertically aligned.

☐**Indents:** the setting of temporary margins within a document differing from the primary margins used.

☐**Centering**text on a line.

☐**Insertion:** the entry of new text within previously typed material without erasing the existing material.

☐**Overstriking:** the substitution of new text for old by typing over the old text.

☐**Deletion:** erasure of text from the screen, or of whole documents from the disk.

☐**Search and Replace:** moving directly to specified words or parts of words within a document and replacing them with different words or word portions.

☐**Copying or Cutting:** the duplication or moving of blocks of text within a document.

☐**Boilerplate:** the separate storage and retrieval of blocks of text from which standard documents can be built.

☐**Pagination:** automatic division of a document into pages of specified numbers of lines.

☐**Page Numbering:** automatic sequential numbering of pages.

☐**Headers and Footers:** option of creating standard blocks of text that will automatically appear at the top or bottom of each page in a document.

☐**Footnoting:** automatic sequential numbering of footnotes and positioning of the footnotes at the bottom of their appropriate pages during pagination.

☐**Table of Contents and Index Generators.** Programs that create these based on the text of a document.

☐**Form Letter Merging:** automatic combining of a form letter with a mailing list to generate multiple copies of the letter with the different addresses and other variable information filled in.

☐**Automatic Spelling Checker and Corrector.** Program that compares words in the text against an on-line dictionary, flagging items not found in the dictionary and offering alternative

Using the Toolbar

The following screen shot shows the WinDbg toolbar.

The toolbar buttons have various effects. Most of them are equivalent to menu commands. To execute the command that is associated with a toolbar button, click the toolbar button. When you ca Hiding the Toolbar or Status Bar

To display or hide the toolbar, select or clear Toolbar on the **View** menu. To display or hide the status bar, select or clear Status Bar on the **View** menu.

If you hide the toolbar or the status bar, you have more space for debugging information windows in the WinDbg display area.

nnot use a button, it appears unavailable.

3.Compare and contrast the terms CD, DVD and Bluraydisk.

CD (Compact Disc)

Compact discs are very low density and have the smallest data storage capability.

You can store about 700 MB of data on most CD's. It doesn't sound like a lot but when I was growing up we only had floppy disc drives which could sore less than 2 MB. When CD's came out we were wrapped and its all anyone could talk about in the computer industry.

DVD (Digital Versatile Disc)

Because of the higher storage capability of DVD's of around 4.2 GB it became the standard for storing Movies on in the 2000's.

Suddenly we had the ability to store all this information we couldn't on a CD. The movie industry jumped on board and before you new it we needed more space and better quality!

You can also store the same information onto DVD's as you can on a CD. The only difference is you can store a lot more.

Blu-ray Discs

Blu-ray discs are a much higher density upgrade on the DVD standard.

With much higher storage capability, up to 128 GB movies and colours appear much more vibrant and audio sounds much more richer. Blu-ray discs get their name from the type of laser needed to burn the data onto the discs which is Blue and Violet.

Blu-ray discs cost more than CD's and DVD's.

Burning CD's, DVD's and Blu-rays

Although all these discs looks very similar on the surface, they are indeed different.

For most of us, we use these discs to read the information on them, but you can also transfer information back the other way to the discs. This process is called burning as a laser is used to facilitate the transfer to the discs.

You can not use a CD burner to burn DVD's and Blu-ray Discs.

Although most DVD burners will be able to burn to CD's as well, for the most part you need a burner specific to the media you are trying to burn to.

Therefore, if you want to be able to burn to Blu-rays and CD or DVD burner wont work. You will need to purchase a Blu-ray burner.

4.Briefly explain the term Internet and the ways to connect to Internet Also discuss the most popular services of Internet.

The **Internet** is the global system of interconnected computernetworks that use the Internet protocol suite (TCP/IP) to link devices worldwide. It is a *network of* *networks* that consists of private, public, academic, business, and government networks of local to global scope, linked by a broad array of electronic, wireless, and optical networking technologies. The Internet carries an extensive range of information resources and services, such as the inter-linked hypertext documents and applications of the World Wide Web (WWW), electronic mail, telephony, and peer-to-peer networks for file sharing.

Dial-up

This is where it all started. You would take your home or office phone handset, and put it into a cradle called a **mod**ulator/**dem**odulator, or modem as we know them today.

The modem took digital signals from your computer and turned them into audible sounds that would get transmitted though the mouthpiece of the handset. Off the signal would go over ordinary telephone wires to the computer that was acting as your Internet service provider. The signal coming back from the Internet would be played into the ear-piece of the phone and the modem would translate that audible signal into a digital signal that the computer could work with.

DSL (Telephone Line)

DSL is an initialization of **D**igital **S**ubscriber **L**ine. The phone companies developed a way to send a second signal down the phone lines, and they did this by sending it at a higher frequency. It's a pretty complex method, but if you're trying to explain it to someone, here's a simplified analogy. Imagine a pipe that you send a green marble down every 60 seconds. When there are green marbles in the pipe, that appears to be all that you can really do with it – send green marbles. Those green marbles are the voice communications.

Cable (Coaxial Cable)

When Internet access made the jump from dial-up, cable was the first new medium to be used. The cable used is the same as the cable that you may have for cable TV. One of those round cables, with a solid copper wire core inside of a thick plastic like insulator. Around the insulator there is usually a foil shield with a braided aluminum jacket around that. All of that is inside the outer plastic jacket of the cable.

Fibre Optic

The technologies that we've talked about so far use electricity and copper wires to transmit the signal. Then along comes fiber optics. In it's simplest terms, the signal is light and the medium is a special type of flexible glass or clear plastic cable. Light actually travels faster than electricity, a *lot* faster, at least when it comes to electricity flowing through a copper wire.

1 Electronic Mail

Used to send electronic message over the internet.

2 Telnet

Used to log on to a remote computer that is attached to internet.

3 Newsgroup

Offers a forum for people to discuss topics of common interests.

4 Internet Relay Chat (IRC)

Allows the people from all over the world to communicate in real time.

Mailing Lists

5 Used to organize group of internet users to share common information through e-mail.

Internet Telephony (VoIP)

6 Allows the internet users to talk across internet to any PC equipped to receive the call.

Instant Messaging

7 Offers real time chat between individuals and group of people. Eg. Yahoo messenger, MSN messenger.

5.What do you mean by the term Data type? Explain in detail the various data Types supported by C++ along with their memory requirement

A data type, in programming, is a classification that specifies which type of value a variable has and what type of mathematical, relational or logical operations can be applied to it without causing an error. A string, for example, is a data type that is used to classify text and an integer is a data type used to classify whole numbers.

Data Type	keyword	Description
Integer Data Type	int	Stores the Integer Value
Float Data Type	float	Stores the Floating Point Value
Character Data Type	char	Stores the Single Character Value
Long Data Type	long	Stores the Long range Integer Value
Double Data Type	double	Stores the long range Floating Value

Explanation :

1. Whenever we declare variable in Computer's memory, Computer must know the **type of the data to be stored inside the memory**.

2. If we need to store the single character then the size of memory occupied will be different than storing the single integer number.

3. The memory in our computers is organized in bytes. A **byte is the minimum amount of memory** that we can manage in C.

4. A byte can store a relatively small amount of data one single character or a small integer (generally an integer between 0 and 255).

Size Required to Store Variable of Different Data Types

Data Type	Borland C/C++ Compiler	Visual C++
Integer	2 Bytes	4 bytes
Float	4 Bytes	4 Bytes
Character	1 Byte	1 Byte
Long	4 Byte	8 Byte

Section-C

6.what is a constructor? How is it defined and when is it called? Also discuss various types of constructors used in C++ programs.

In class-basedobject-oriented programming, a **constructor** (abbreviation: **ctor**) in a class is a special type of subroutine called to create an object. It prepares the new object for use, often accepting arguments that the constructor uses to set required member variables.

A constructor resembles an instance method, but it differs from a method in that it has no explicit return type, it is not implicitly inherited and it usually has different rules for scope modifiers. Constructors often have the same name as the declaring class. They have the task of initializing the object's data members and of establishing the invariant of the class, failing if the invariant is invalid. A properly written constructor leaves the resulting object in a *valid* state. Immutable objects must be initialized in a constructor.

Types

Parameterized constructors

Constructors that can take at least one argument are termed as parameterized constructors. For example:

```
classExample
{
intx,y;
public:
Example();
Example(inta,intb);// Parameterized constructor
};
Example::Example()
{
}
Example::Example(inta,intb)
{
x=a;
y=b;
}
```

When an object is declared in a parameterized constructor, the initial values have to be passed as arguments to the constructor function. The normal way of object declaration may not work. The constructors can be called explicitly or implicitly. The method of calling the constructor implicitly is also called the *shorthand* method.

Examplee=Example(0,50);// Explicit call

Examplee(0,50);// Implicit call

Default constructors

If the programmer does not supply a constructor for an instantiable class, most languages will provide a *default constructor*.

The behavior of the default constructor is language dependent. It may initialize data members to zero or other same values, or it may do nothing at all.

Some languages (Java, C#, VB .NET) will default construct arrays of class types to contain null references. Languages without null references may not allow default construction of arrays of non default constructible objects, or require explicit initialization at the time of the creation (C++):

#include<iostream>

```
classstudent{
public:
inta,b;
student(a=0,b=0)//default constructor
};
intmain(){
}
```

Copy constructors

Copy constructors define the actions performed by the compiler when copying class objects. A copy constructor has one formal parameter that is the type of the class (the parameter may be a reference to an object). It is used to create a copy of an existing object of the same class. Even though both classes are the same, it counts as a conversion constructor.

While copy constructors are usually abbreviated **copy ctor** or **cctor**, they have nothing to do with *class constructors* used in .NET using the same abbreviation.

7 a) What are Functions? Write a program to find maximum of three variables.

Functions are what we use to describe things we want to talk about mathematically. I find, though, that I get a bit tongue tied when I try to define them.

The simplest definition is: **a function is a bunch of ordered pairs of things (in our case the things will be numbers, but they can be otherwise), with the property that the first members of the pairs are all d**The general form of a C++ function definition is as follows:

```
return_typefunction_name( parameter list ){
body of the function
}
```

A C++ function definition consists of a function header and a function body. Here are all the parts of a function:

- **Return Type**: A function may return a value. The **return_type** is the data type of the value the function returns. Some functions perform the desired operations without returning a value. In this case, the return_type is the keyword **void**.

- **Function Name:** This is the actual name of the function. The function name and the parameter list together constitute the function signature.

- **Parameters:** A parameter is like a placeholder. When a function is invoked, you pass a value to the parameter. This value is referred to as actual parameter or argument. The parameter list refers to the type, order, and number of the parameters of a function. Parameters are optional; that is, a function may contain no parameters.

- **Function Body:** The function body contains a collection of statements that define what the function does.

Example

Following is the source code for a function called **max()**. This function takes two parameters num1 and num2 and returns the maximum between the two:

```
// function returning the max between two numbers

int max(int num1,int num2){
// local variable declaration
int result;

if(num1 > num2)
result= num1;
else
result= num2;

return result;
}
```

Function Declarations

A function **declaration** tells the compiler about a function name and how to call the function. The actual body of the function can be defined separately.

A function declaration has the following parts:

```
return_typefunction_name( parameter list );
```

For the above defined function max(), following is the function declaration:

```
int max(int num1, int num2);
```

Parameter names are not importan in function declaration only their type is required, so following is also valid declaration:

```
int max(int, int);
```

Function declaration is required when you define a function in one source file and you call that function in another file. In such case, you should declare the function at the top of the file calling the function.

Calling a Function

While creating a C++ function, you give a definition of what the function has to do. To use a function, you will have to call or invoke that function.

When a program calls a function, program control is transferred to the called function. A called function performs defined task and when its return statement is executed or when its function-ending closing brace is reached, it returns program control back to the main program.

To call a function, you simply need to pass the required parameters along with function name, and if function returns a value, then you can store returned value. For example:

```
#GREATEST OF THREE NUMBERS
#include<stdio.h>
int main()
{
double n1, n2, n3;

printf("Enter three numbers: ");
scanf("%lf %lf %lf",&n1,&n2,&n3);

if( n1>=n2 && n1>=n3 )
printf("%.2f is the largest number.", n1);

if( n2>=n1 && n2>=n3 )
printf("%.2f is the largest number.", n2);
```

```
if( n3>=n1 && n3>=n2 )
printf("%.2f is the largest number.", n3);


return0;
}
```

(b) Define the term pointer. Write a program to compare pointerthe two given strings using a pointer.

A pointer is a variable which contains the address in memory of another variable. We can have a pointer to any variable type.

The *unary* or *monadic* operator **&** gives the ``address of a variable".

The *indirection* or dereference operator * gives the ``contents of an object *pointed to* by a pointer".

To declare a pointer to a variable do:

```
  int *pointer;
```

int x = 1, y = 2;

       int *ip;

       ip = &x;

y = *ip;

x = ip;

       *ip = 3;

It is worth considering what is going on at the ***machine level*** in memory to fully understand how pointer work. Consider Fig. 9.1. Assume for the sake of this discussion that variable x resides at memory location 100, y at 200 and ip at 1000. **Note** A pointer is a variable and thus its values need to be stored somewhere. It is the nature of the pointers value that is ***new***.

```
int x = 1, y =2;
int *ip;

ip = &x;
```

x	1		y	2		ip	100
	100			200			1000

```
y = *ip;
```

x	1		y	1		ip	100
	100			200			1000

```
x = ip;
```

x	100		y	1		ip	100
	100			200			1000

```
*ip = 3
```

x	3		y	1		ip	100
	100			200			1000

```
1.    #include<stdio.h>
2.
3.    intcompare_string(char*, char*);
4.
5.    main()
6.    {
7.        char first[100], second[100], result;
8.
9.    printf("Enter first string\n");
10.       gets(first);
11.
12.   printf("Enter second string\n");
13.       gets(second);
14.
15.       result = compare_string(first, second);
16.
17.       if ( result == 0 )
18.   printf("Both strings are same.\n");
19.       else
20.   printf("Entered strings are not equal.\n");
21.
22.       return 0;
23.   }
24.
25.   intcompare_string(char *first, char *second)
26.   {
```

```
27.    while(*first==*second)
28.    {
29.        if ( *first == '\0' || *second == '\0' )
30.            break;
31.
32.        first++;
33.        second++;
34.    }
35.    if( *first == '\0' && *second == '\0' )
36.        return 0;
37.    else
38.        return -1;
39.  }
40.
```

9.   a)Explain how data member and data functions of base class can be accessed by the derived class member functions.

Member functions can (and should) be used to interact with data contained within user defined types. User defined types provide flexibility in the "*divide and conquer*" scheme in program writing. In other words, one programmer can write a user defined type and guarantee an interface. Another programmer can write the main program with that expected interface. The two pieces are put together and compiled for usage. User defined types provide *encapsulation* defined in the Object Oriented Programming (OOP) paradigm.

An object may contain values which are stored internally and are unique to that object. In order to do this, each value needs an appropriate declaration as a data member in the class. A data member may be of any type, including classes already defined, pointers to objects of any type, or even references to objects of any type.

Data members may be private or public, but are usually held private so that values may only be changed at the discretion of the class function members. In the example below, the class C contains two a private data member of type int, and a public data member of type pointer to char.

There is no other way to access other class's private data then friendship. What you can do with inheritance, however, is to access protected data of the base class. But it doesn't mean you can access protected data of another object of the base type. You can only access protected data of the*base part* of the derived class:

class base{

protected://protected instead of private

```
base*ptr1;
int data;
public:
base(){}
base(int d){ data=d;}
};

classderived:private base{
public:
void member();
};

void derived::member()
{
base*temp=new base(3);
//temp->ptr1 = 0; //you need friendship to access ptr1 in temp

this->ptr1 =0;// but you can access base::ptr1 while it is protected
}
```

b)what is meant by membership operator in c++.

he . (dot) operator and the -> (arrow) operator are used to reference individual members of classes, structures, and unions.

The dot operator is applied to the actual object. The arrow operator is used with a pointer to an object. For example, consider the following structure:

```
structEmployee{
charfirst_name[16];
int  age;
}emp;
```

The (.) dot operator

To assign the value "zara" to the **first_name** member of object emp, you would write something as follows:

```
strcpy(emp.first_name, "zara");
```

The (->) arrow operator

If p_emp is a pointer to an object of type Employee, then to assign the value "zara" to the **first_name** member of object emp, you would write something as follows:

```
strcpy(p_emp->first_name, "zara");
```

The -> is called the arrow operator. It is formed by using the minus sign followed by a greater than sign.

Simply saying: To access members of a structure, use the dot operator. To access members of a structure through a pointer, use the arrow operator.

The statement p->m is interpreted as (p.operator->())->m. Using the same concept, following example explains how a class access operator -> can be overloaded.

```cpp
#include<iostream>
#include<vector>
usingnamespacestd;

// Consider an actual class.
classObj{
staticinti, j;

public:
void f()const{cout<<i++<<endl;}
void g()const{cout<<j++<<endl;}
};

// Static member definitions:
intObj::i=10;
intObj::j =12;
```

```
// Implement a container for the above class
classObjContainer{
vector<Obj*> a;
public:
void add(Obj*obj){
a.push_back(obj);// call vector's standard method.
}
friendclassSmartPointer;
};


// implement smart pointer to access member of Obj class.
classSmartPointer{
ObjContaineroc;
int index;
public:
SmartPointer(ObjContainer&objc){
oc=objc;
index=0;
}


// Return value indicates end of list:
booloperator++()// Prefix version {
if(index >=oc.a.size())returnfalse;
if(oc.a[++index]==0)returnfalse;
returntrue;
}
booloperator++(int)// Postfix version {
returnoperator++();
}
```

```
// overload operator->
Obj*operator->()const{
if(!oc.a[index]){
cout<<"Zero value";
return(Obj*)0;
}
returnoc.a[index];
}
};
int main(){
constintsz=10;
Objo[sz];
ObjContaineroc;

for(inti=0;i<sz;i++){
oc.add(&o[i]);
}
SmartPointersp(oc);// Create an iterator
do{
sp->f();// smart pointer call
sp->g();
}while(sp++);
return0;
}
```

9.What is Random Access File and how it is defined in C++. Write a program to read students' record such as name, roll no, height and weight from specified file and to display in sorted order using roll no as a key for sorting.

In C++, random access is achieved by manipulating seekg(), seekp(), tellg() and tellp() functions. The seekg() and tellg() functions allow you to set and examine the get_pointer, and the seekp() and tellp() functions perform these operations on the put_pointer.

The seekg() and tellg() functions are for input streams (ifstream) and seekp() and tellp() functions are for output streams (ofstream). However, if you use them with an fstreamobject then tellg() and tellp() return the same value. Also seekg() and seekp() work the same way in an fstream object. seekg() and tellg() functions are for input streams (ifstream) and seekp() and tellp() functions are for output streams (ofstream). However, if you use them with an fstream object then tellg() and tellp() return the same value. Also seekg() and seekp() work the same way in an fstream object. The most common forms of these functions are :

seekg()	istream&seekg(long); istream&seekg(long, seek_dir);	Form 1 Form 2
seekp()	ofstream&seekp(long); ofstream&seekp(long, seek_dir);	Form 1 Form 2
tellg()	long tellg()	
tellp()	long tellp()	

The working of seekg() &seekp() and tellg() &tellp() is just the same except that seekg() and tellg() work for ifstream objects and seekp() and tellp() work for ofstream objects. In the above table, seek_dir takes the definition enumseek_dir{ beg, cur, end};.

The seekg() or seekp(), when used according to Form 1, then it moves the get_pointer or put_pointer to an absolute position. Here is an example:

ifstream fin;

ofstreamfout;

:   // file opening routine

fin.seekg(30);   // will move the get_pointer (in ifstream) to byte number 30 in the file

fout.seekp(30);   // will move the put_pointer (in ofstream) to byte number 30 in the file

When seekg() or seekp() function is used according to Form 2, then it moves the get_pointer or put_pointer to a position relative to the current position, following the definition of seek_dir. Since, seek_dir is an enumeration defined in the header file iostream.h, that has the following values:

ios::beg,   // refers to the beginning of the file

ios::cur,   // refers to the current position in the file

ios::end}   // refers to the end of the file

Here is an example.

fin.seekg(30, ios::beg); // go to byte no. 30 from beginning of file linked with fin

fin.seekg(-2, ios::cur);   // back up 2 bytes from the current position of get pointer

fin.seekg(0, ios::end);   // go to the end of the file

fin.seekg(-4, ios::end);   // backup 4 bytes from the end of the file

The functions tellg() and tellp() return the position, in terms of byte number, of put_pointer and get_pointer respectively, in an output file and input file.

Using file streams, we can randomly access binary files. By random access, you can go to any position in the file as you wish (instead of going in a sequential order from the first character to the last). Earlier in this chapter we discussed about a bookmarker that will keep moving as you keep reading a file. This bookmarker will move sequentially but you can also make it move randomly using some functions. Technically this bookmarker is a file pointer and it determines as to where to write the next character (or from where to read the next character). We have seen that file streams can be created for input (ifstream) or for output (ofstream). For ifstream the pointer is called as 'get' pointer and for ofstream the pointer is called as 'put' pointer. fstream can perform both input and output operations and hence it has one 'get' pointer and one 'put' pointer. The 'get' pointer indicates the byte number in the file from where the next input has to occur. The 'put' pointer indicates the byte number in the file where the next output has to be made. There are two functions to enable you move these pointers in a file wherever you want to:

seekg ( ) - belongs to the ifstream class
seekp ( ) - belongs to the ofstream class

We'll write a program to copy the string "Hi this is a test file" into a file called mydoc.txt. Then we'll attempt to read the file starting from the 8th character (using the seekg( ) function).

Strings are character arrays terminated in a null character ('\0'). If you want to copy a string of text into a character array, you should make use of the function:

strcpy (*character-array, text*);

to copy the text into the character array (even blank spaces will be copied into the character array). To make use of this function you might need to include the string.h header file.

```cpp
#include <iostream.h>
#include <fstream.h>
#include <string.h>

int main( )
{
ofstream out("c:/mydoc.txt",ios::binary);
char text[80];
strcpy(text,"Hi this is a test file");
out<<text;
out.close( );
ifstream in("c:/mydoc.txt",ios::binary);
in.seekg(8);
cout<<endl<<"Starting from position 8 the contents are:"<<endl;

while ( !in.eof( ) )
{
char ch;
in.get(ch);
if ( !in.eof( ) )
    {
    cout<<ch;
    }
}

in.close( );
return 0;
}
```

EXAMINATION MAY-2014

FUNDAMENTALS OF COMPUTER PROGRAMMING & IT

BTCS-101 PAPER ID-A1108

SECTION-A

1. **Give short answer of the following:**

a. **What is an operating system?**

An **operating system (OS)** is system software that manages computer hardware and software resources and provides common services for computer programs. the operating system acts as an intermediary between programs and the computer hardwareThe dominant desktop operating system is Microsoft Windows , macOS by Apple Inc. and Linux In the mobile (smartphone and tablet combined) sector, Android by Google , iOS by Apple. Linux is dominant in the server and supercomputing sectors.

b. **Differenciate between primary memory and secondary memory.**

Primary memory is the internal working memory of a computer, and it includes RAM and the cache. Secondary storage is also called external memory, and it includes the computer's hard drive.

c. **What are keywords?**

In C++, keywords are reserved identifiers which cannot be used as names for the variables in a program.eg. main,if,else,int,void,switch,while etc.. Keywords cannot be used for the –Declaring Variable Name, Declaring Class Name, Declaring Function Name, Declaring Object Name

d. **What are Expressions? How are they evaluated?**

An expression is a sequence of operators and their operands, that specifies a computation. "Expression in C++ is form when we combine operands (variables and constant) and C++ OPERATORS". "Evaluation" mostly means "simplifying an expression down to a single numerical value". Sometimes you will be given a numerical expression, where all you have todo is simplify; that is more of an order-of-operations kind of question. Every expression consists of at least one *operand* and can have one or more *operators*. Operands are values, whereas operators are symbols that represent particular actions. In the expression x + 5

x and 5 are operands, and + is an operator.At first, the expressions within parenthesis are evaluated. If no parenthesis is present, then the arithmetic expression is evaluated from left to right. There are two priority levels of operators in C.

High priority: * / %

Low priority: + -

e.   What is the use of continue statement?

Continue statement is mostly used inside loops. Whenever it is encountered inside a loop, control directly jumps to the beginning of the loop for next iteration, skipping the execution of **statements** inside loop's body for the current iteration.

f.   Differentiate between library functions and user defined functions.

Functions are of two type:-

Built in function or Library Functions

User defined functions

Library Functions: Built in functions are the functions that are provided by C library. Many activities in C are carried out using library functions. These functions perform file access, mathematical computations, graphics, memory management etc. A library function is accessed simply by writing the function name, followed by an optional list of arguments and header file of used function should be included with the program. Definition of built in functions are defined in a special header file. A header file can contain definition of more than one library function but the same function can not be defined in two header files.

User defined function:- Functions provided by library are not enough for user so to complete their needs user has to define some functions themselves, these are called user defined functions. Means except built in functions user can also define and write small programs as functions to do a task relevant to their programs, there functions should be codified by the user, so that such functions can perform the task as desired by user.

g.   what is Data encapsulation?

Data encapsulation sometimes referred to as **data** hiding, is the mechanism whereby the implementation details of a class are kept hidden from the user. The user can only perform a restricted set of operations on the hidden members of the class by executing special functions commonly called methods.

h.   What are constructors?

Constructors are special class functions which performs initialization of every object. The Compiler calls the Constructor whenever an object is created. Constructors iitialize values to object members after storage is allocated to the object.

class A

```
{
int x;
public:
A(); //Constructor
};
```

While defining a contructor you must remeber that the name of constructor will be same as the name of the class, and contructors never have return type.

What is a friend function ?

Private data members cannot be accessed from outside the class. However, situations arise where two classes need to share a particular function. To allow a non-member function the access to private members of a class, it needs to be friend of that class. If a function is defined as a friend function then, the private and protected data of a class can be accessed using the <u>function</u>. For accessing the data, the declaration of a friend function should be made inside the body of the class (can be anywhere inside class either in private or public section) starting with keyword friend. Declaration of friend function in C++

class class_name

```
{
    ... .. ...
    friend return_type function_name(argument/s);
    ... .. ...
}
```

i.   What is a stream?

SECTION-B

II.   Draw and explain the components of block diagram of the computer.

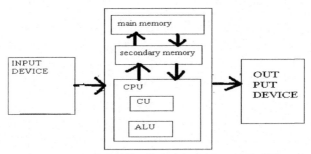

BLOCK DIAGRAM OF A DIGITAL COMPUTER

Input device : In put device is the device by which we can send some thing (data) to computer from out side of the computer. Example of input Device : Mouse, Keyboard, Scanner, light pen, joystick etc.

Out put device : This device send the result done by the computer to the outer world or to the user (out side the computer). Example: Monitor,Printer, Speaker etc.

Memory : Mainly Computer has two types of memory.

i) Main or primary memory: High speed memory used to control the data input or output speed with the processor speed. Size of main memory is small. Cost is high.

ii) Secondary Memory : Speed of this memory is slow. But We can use a vest amount of secondary memory to story long size data. Cost of Secondary memory is low.

Example: main memory --- RAM / ROM (Random access memory / Read only memory)

Secondary Memory : HDD (Hard disk Drive), FDD (Floppy Disk Drive), Pen drive, Memory Chip etc.

There is another type of super speed memory called CASH Memory. It is kind of Main memory (Some body called cash memory is a main memory, some body called CASH memory is a new type of memory. But from my view it is main memory).

CPU : Central Processing Unit is the hart of the Computer. With out CPU computer is nothing. It is a chip or IC (Integrated Circuit). Control control the whole process of the computer. It has two main part

i) CU (Control Unit) : This part generate the control signal for all device which is connected with a computer.

ii) ALU (Arithmetic Logic Unit) : All types of calculation (like ADD, SUB,DIV,MULT, OR,AND etc) done in this unit.

III. What do you mean by GUI? What are the significant features of GUI based operating system.

Graphical User Interface (GUI) is a system that allows users to interact with computers. GUI is not an operating system, but rather an interface design on your computer, so computer that you use has a more attractive appearance than the computer a few decades ago.

A graphical user interface contains six important features, including a pointer, pointing device, icons, desktop, windows and menus. A GUI denotes a collection of computer programs that utilize a computer's graphics capabilities to make programs easier to use. **Pointer:** A symbol that appears on the <u>display screen</u> and that you move to <u>select</u> <u>objects</u> and <u>commands</u>. Usually, the pointer appears as a small angled arrow. <u>Text</u> -processing <u>applications</u>, however, use an *I-beam pointer* that is shaped like a capital *I*.

The significant features of GUI based operating system.

Pointing device: A <u>device</u>, such as a <u>mouse</u> or <u>trackball</u>, that enables you to select objects on the display screen.

Icons: Small pictures that represent commands, <u>files</u>, or <u>windows</u>. By moving the pointer to the icon and pressing a <u>mouse button</u>, you can <u>execute</u> a command or <u>convert</u> the icon into a window. You can also move the icons around the display screen as if they were real objects on your desk.

Desktop: The area on the display screen where icons are grouped is often referred to as the desktop because the icons are intended to represent real objects on a real desktop.

Windows: You can divide the screen into different areas. In each window, you can <u>run</u> a different program or display a different file. You can move windows around the display screen, and change their shape and size at will.

Menus: Most graphical user interfaces let you execute commands by selecting a choice from a menu. In addition to their visual components, graphical user interfaces also make it easier to move <u>data</u> from one application to another. A true GUI includes standard <u>formats</u> for representing text and graphics. Because the formats are well-defined, different programs that run under a common GUI can share data. This makes it possible, for example, to <u>copy</u> a graph created by a <u>spreadsheet program</u> into a <u>document</u> created by a <u>word processor</u>.

Many <u>DOS</u> programs include some <u>features</u> of GUIs, such as menus, but are not *graphics based*. Such interfaces are sometimes called *graphical <u>character-based</u> user interfaces* to distinguish them from true GUIs.

IV.   Define an algorithm. Write an algorithm to check whether a given no. is prime or not. Draw its flow chart as well.

In programming, algorithm are the set of well defined instruction in sequence to solve a program. An algorithm should always have a clear stopping point.

Qualities of a good algorithm

1. Inputs and outputs should be defined precisely.

2. Each steps in algorithm should be clear and unambiguous.

3. Algorithm should be most effective among many different ways to solve a problem.

4. An algorithm shouldn't have computer code. Instead, the algorithm should be written in such a way that, it can be used in similar programming languages.

An algorithm to check whether a number entered by user is prime or not.

Step 1: Start

Step 2: Declare variables n,i,flag.

Step 3: Initialize variables

   flag$\leftarrow$1

   i$\leftarrow$2

Step 4: Read n from user.

Step 5: Repeat the steps until i<(n/2)

   5.1 If remainder of n÷i equals 0

      flag$\leftarrow$0

      Go to step 6

   5.2 i$\leftarrow$i+1

Step 6: If flag=0

      Display n is not prime

   else

      Display n is prime

Step 7: Stop

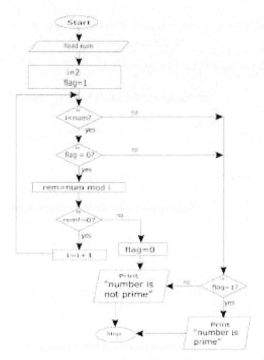

V.   What are spreadsheets? How are they created? Describe how data in a spreadsheet can be analyzed by using simple graphs like bar charts and line graphs.

Alternatively referred to as a **worksheet**, a **spreadsheet** is a file made of <u>rows</u> and <u>columns</u> that help sort data, arrange data easily, and calculate <u>numerical</u> data. What makes a spreadsheet <u>software</u> program unique is its ability to calculate values using mathematical <u>formulas</u> and the data in <u>cells</u>.

1. Load Microsoft Excel. Click the "File" or "Office" button (it varies according to your version of Excel) on the main menu. Select "New" from the list of options, which brings up a dialog box.

2. Select "Blank Workbook" or a similar option from the list of new file options—it commonly appears as an initial option in the dialog box by default. Click "Create" or "OK" to open the new Excel workbook.

3. Proceed to enter your data into the cells of the worksheets. Three worksheets will appear by default (in most versions). You can toggle between the worksheets using the named tabs at the bottom of the workbook.

4. As another alternative to opening a new workbook, click "CTRL + N" on your keyboard after loading Excel.

Data in a spreadsheet can be analyzed by using simple graphs like bar charts and line graphs.

1. Enter your data into the Excel spreadsheet in table format.

2. With your cursor, highlight the cells that contain the information that you want to appear in your graph.

3. With the text selected, click Insert → Chart.

SECTION - C

VI. a) What is reference variable? What is its major use?

A reference variable is an alias, that is, another name for an already existingvariable. Once a reference is initialized with a variable, either the variable name or the reference name may be used to refer to the variable.

C++ objects lifetime could be automatic (within local or global scope) or manual (explicitly allocated/deallocated in heap). C++ reference is just simple alias for an object. ... A reference is a pointer with restrictions. A reference is a way of accessing an object, but is not the object itself.

b) Differentiate between call by value and call by reference.

On the basis of arguments there are two types of function are available in C++ language, they are;

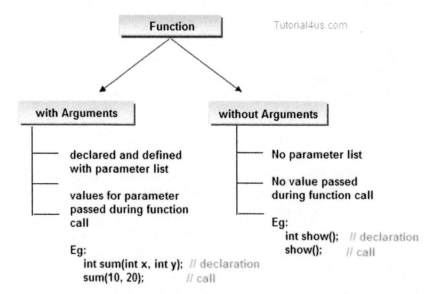

- With argument

- Without argument

If a function take any arguments, it must declare variables that accept the values as a arguments. These variables are called the formal parameters of the function. There are two ways to pass value or data to function in C++ language which is given below;

- call by value

- call by reference

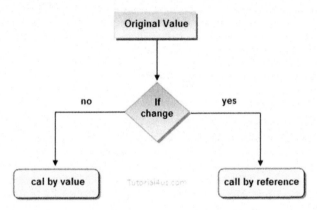

Call by value

In call by value, **original value can not be changed** or modified. In call by value, when you passed value to the function it is locally stored by the function parameter in stack memory location. If you change the value of function parameter, it is changed for the current function only but it not change the value of variable inside the caller function such as main().

Call by reference

In call by reference, **original value is changed** or modified because we pass reference (address). Here, address of the value is passed in the function, so actual and formal arguments shares the same address space. Hence, any value changed inside the function, is reflected inside as well as outside the function.

VII   a) What is a class? How does it accomplish data hiding.

A **class** in C++ is a user defined type or data structure declared with keyword **class**that has data and functions (also called methods) as its members whose access is governed by the three access specifiers private, protected or public (by default access to members of a **class** is private).

Data Hiding: In object oriented programming most of the item data members is defined as private and member function will be defined as public. The public members of the class can be accessed from inside of the class as well as from the outside of the class. The private members of the class can be accessed from inside of the class but cannot be accessed from outside of the class. Thus private members remain hidden from outside of the class. Since most of the time the data members are kept private it remains hidden from outside of the class and thus the data hiding is implemented. Since data members are private the class user cannot access them directly but ca access them through predefined functions.

There are three types of access specifier.They are

- Private :Within the block.

- Public:Whole over the class.

- Protected:Act as a public and then act as a private.

Within a class members can be declared as either public protected or private in order to explicitly enforce encapsulation. The elements placed after the public keyword is accessible to all the user of the class.

The elements placed after the protected keyword is accessible only to the methods of the class. The elements placed after the private keyword are accessible only to the methods of the class. The data is hidden inside the class by declaring it as private inside the class. Thus private data cannot be directly accessed by the object.

General Form:
class class name
{
private:
datatype data;
public:
Member functions;
};
main()
{
classname objectname1,objectname2...............;
}
Example:
class Square
{
private:

int Num;
public:
void Get() {
  cout<<"Enter Number:";
  cin>>Num;
}
void Display() {
  *cout<<"Square Is:"<<Num*Num;*
}
};
void main()
{
Square Obj;
Obj.Get();
Obj.Display();
getch()
}

b)   Can we have more than one constructor in a class? If yes, explain the need of such situation.

Yes, a class in C++ can have more than one constructor with the same name. this interesting feature of the constructor is known as constructor overloading. All the constructors have the same name as the corresponding class but differ only in terms of their signature (in terms of the number of arguments, or data types of their arguments, or both) as shown in the below program.

```
#include<iostream.h>
Class Account
{
Private :
Int acc_no;
Float balance ;
Public :
Account ( )
```

VIII. What does inheritance mean in C++? What are the different forms of inheritance?

Inheritance in Object Oriented Programming can be described as a process of creating new classes from existing classes. New classes **inherit** some of the properties and behavior of the existing classes. An existing class that is "parent" of a new class is called a base class. ... **Inheritance** is a technique of code reuse.

Types of Inheritance

- Single Inheritance.

- Multiple Inheritance.

- Hierarchical Inheritance.

- Multilevel Inheritance.

- Hybrid Inheritance (also known as Virtual Inheritance)

IX.   What is file? Write a program that read some text form the keyboard and write it into a file named"Abc.txt". The program then read this file and display its contents on the computer screen.

Sometime, it is important to store the information entered by the user into the file for further use. After storing the information into the file, later you can retrieve those information from that file. File helps in storing the information permanently. A file itself is a bunch of bytes stored on some storage devices like taps, or magnet disk etc. In C++, the file input/output operation are performed through a component header file fstream.h of C++ standard library. In C++, a file

- at its lowest level - is interpreted simply as a sequence, or stream, of bytes.

- at the user level - consists of a sequence of intermixed data types such as characters, arithmetic values, class objects

The fstream.h library predefines a set of operations for handling file related input and output operation. It defines certain classes that helps in performing the file input and output operations. The transfer of input - data or output - data from one computer to another can be easily done by using files.

```
/* C++ File Handling - This is the complete
 * version of the C++ file handling program.
 * This program creates a file (entered by user)
 * and store some content (entered by user).
 * Then display those content (if user want)
 * on the output screen in C++ */
#include<iostream.h>
#include<conio.h>
#include<fstream.h>
#include<stdlib.h>
void main()
{
        char rec[80], ch;
```

```cpp
char fname[20];
int count=0, i;
char ans='y';
clrscr();

cout<<"Enter file name: ";
cin.get(fname, 20);
ofstream fout(fname, ios::out);

if(!fout)
{
        cout<<"Error in creating the file..!!\n";
        cout<<"Press any key to exit...\n";
        getch();
        exit(1);
}
cin.get(ch);

cout<<"Enter information to store..\n";
while(ans=='y' || ans=='Y')
{
        cin.get(rec, 80);
        fout<<rec<<"\n";
        cout<<"Want to enter more ? (y/n).. ";
        cin>>ans;
        count++;
        cin.get(ch);
}
cout<<"\nThe information successfully stored in the file..!!\n";
fout.close();

cin.get(ch);
cout<<"Want to see ? (y/n)..";
cin>>ans;

if(ans=='y' || ans=='Y')
{
        ifstream fin(fname, ios::in);
        if(!fin)
```

```
            {
                    cout<<"Error in opening the file..!!\n";
                    cout<<"Press any key to exit..\n";
                    getch();
                    exit(2);
            }
            fin.seekg(0);
            cout<<"\n";

            cout<<"The file contains:\n";
            for(i=0; i<count; i++)
            {
                    fin.get(rec, 80);
                    fin.get(ch);
                    cout<<rec<<"\n";
            }
            fin.close();
    }

    getch();
}
```

Roll No. ....

Total No. of Questions : 09]   [Total No. of Pages : 02

B.Tech. (Sem.-1ˢᵗ/2ⁿᵈ)

FUNDAMENTALS OF COMPUTER PROGRAMMING AND IT

SUBJECT CODE: BTCS-101(2011 and 2012 batch)

PAPER ID: [A1108]

Time: 03 Hours   Maximum Marks : 60

Instruction to Candidates :

1)   Section – A is **Compulsory** consisting of **Ten** questions carrying **Two**
marks each.

2)   Section – B and C have **FOUR** questions each.

3)   Attempt any **FIVE** questions from Section – B and C carrying **8** Marks
each.

4)   Select at least **TWO** questions from Section – B and C.

Section –A

Q1) Answer briefly :

a) What do you mean by pseudocode?

Ans: Pseudocode is a detailed yet readable description of what a computer
program or algorithm must do, expressed in a formally-styled natural language
rather than in a programming language. Pseudocode is sometimes used as a
detailed step in the process of developing a program. It allows designers or lead
programmers to express the design in great detail and provides programmers a
detailed template for the next step of writing code in a specific programming
language.

b) Differentiate between RAM and ROM.

Ans: RAM and ROM both are different types of memory and they both store data
in a computer.

Comparison chart of RAM and ROM		
	RAM	**ROM**
1.	Stands for Randon-access Memory	Stands for Read-only memory

2.	RAM is a read and write memory	Normally ROM is read only memory and it can not be overwritten. However, EPROMs can be reprogrammed
3.	RAM is faster	ROM is relatively slower than RAM
4.	RAM is a **volatile memory**. It means that the data in RAM will be lost if power supply is cut-off	ROM is permanent memory. Data in ROM will stay as it is even if we remove the power-supply
5.	There are mainly two types of RAM; static RAM and Dynamic RAM	There are several types of ROM; Erasable ROM, Programmable ROM, EPROM etc.
6.	RAM stores all the applications and data when the computer is up and running	ROM usually stores instructions that are required for starting (booting) the computer
7.	Price of RAM is comparatively high	ROM chips are comparatively cheaper
8.	RAM chips are bigger in size	ROM chips are smaller in size
9.	Processor can directly access the content of RAM	Content of ROM are usually first transferred to RAM and then accessed by processor. This is done in order to be able to access ROM content at a faster speed.
10.	RAM is often installed with large storage.	Storage capacity of ROM installed in a computer is much lesser than RAM

c) List various types of operating system.

Ans: Batch Operating System: Batch operating system is the operating system which analyzes your input and groups them into batches i.e. data in each batch is of similar characteristics. And then it performs operation on each individual batch.

2. Real-time: A real-time operating system is a multitasking operating system that aims at executing real-time applications. Real-time operating systems often use specialized scheduling algorithms so that they can achieve a deterministic nature of behavior..

3. Multi-user vs. Single-user: A multi-user operating system allows multiple users to access a computer system concurrently. Time-sharing system can be classified as multi-user systems as they enable a multiple user access to a computer through the sharing of time. Single-user operating systems, as opposed to a multi-user operating system, are usable by a single user at a time.

4. Multi-tasking vs. Single-tasking: When a single program is allowed to run at a time, the system is grouped under a single-tasking system, while in case the operating system allows the execution of multiple tasks at one time, it is classified as a multi-tasking operating system.

5. Single-processor Systems: On a single-processor system, there is one main CPU capable of executing a general-purpose instruction set, including instructions from user processes.

6. Multi-processor Systems: A multiprocessing operating system allows a program to run on more than one central processing unit (CPU) at a time. This can come in very handy in some work environments, at schools, and even for some home-computing situations.

7. Distributed: A distributed operating system manages a group of independent computers and makes them appear to be a single computer. The development of networked computers that could be linked and communicate with each other, gave rise to distributed computing.

8. Embedded: Embedded operating systems are designed to be used in embedded computer systems. They are designed to operate on small machines like PDAs with less autonomy. They are able to operate with a limited number of resources.

d) What are symbolic constants? How are they created?

Ans: A **symbolic constant** is name that substitute for a sequence of character that cannot be changed. The character may represent a numeric constant, a character constant, or a string. When the program is compiled, each occurrence of a symbolic constant is replaced by its corresponding character sequence. They are usually defined at the beginning of the program. The symbolic constants may then appear later in the program in place of the numeric constants, character constants, etc., that the symbolic constants represent.

Symbolic constant is a quantity which does not change during the execution of the program. Constant qualifiers are keywords used to define a quantity as symbolic constant. The qualifiers are:

1) const.

2) enum.

e) Define Expression.

Ans: An **expression** in a programming language is a combination of one or more explicit values, constants, variables, operators, and functions that the programming language interprets and computes to produce another value.

f) List various advantages of using functions.

Ans: A function is a routine or a set of instruction or code that performs a specific task and can be processed independently.

Advantages of Functions:

i) The length of a source program can be reduced by using functions at appropriate places. This factor is particularly critical with microcomputers where memory space is limited.

ii) It is easy to locate and isolate a faulty function for further investigations.

iii) A function may be used by many other programs. This means that a C programmer can build on what others have already done, instead of starting all over again from scratch.

iv) It facilitates top-down modular programming. In this programming style, the high level logic of the overall problem is solved first while the details of each lower-level function are addressed later.

v) Its interface to the rest of the program is clean and narrow.

g) Differentiate between call by value and call by reference.

Ans: Call by value

In call by value, original value can not be changed **or** modified. In call by value, when you passed value to the function it is locally stored by the function parameter in stack memory location. If you change the value of function parameter, it is changed for the current function only but it not change the value of variable inside the caller function such as main().

Call by reference

In call by reference, original value is changed or modified because we pass reference (address). Here, address of the value is passed in the function, so actual and formal arguments shares the same address space. Hence, any value changed inside the function, is reflected inside as well as outside the function.

h) What do you mean by data encapsulation?

Ans: Encapsulation means that the internal representation of an object is generally hidden from view outside of the object's definition. Typically, only the object's own methods can directly inspect or manipulate its fields.Encapsulation is the hiding of data implementation by restricting access to accessors and mutators.

i) What are constructors?

Ans: Constructors are special class functions which performs initialization of every object. The Compiler calls the Constructor whenever an object is created. Constructors iitialize values to object members after storage is allocated to the object.

class A

{

  int x;

  public:

  A(); //Constructor

};

While defining a constructor you must remember that the name of constructor will be same as the name of the class, and constructors never have return type.

Constructors can be defined either inside the class definition or outside class definition using class name and scope resolution :: operator.

j) Define file.

Ans: A file is an object on a computer that stores data, information, settings, or commands used with a computer program. A collection of data or information that has a name, called the filename. Almost all information stored in a computer must be in a file. There are many different types of files: data files, text files, program files, directory files, and so on. Different types of files store different types of information. For example, program files store programs, whereas text files store text.

Section B

Q2) With the help of a block diagram, describe in detail various components of a computer system.

Ans: A computer is a fast and accurate device, which can accept data, store data, process them and give, desired results as output. The computer is organized into four units as shown in the following diagram.

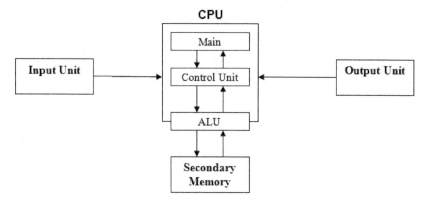

1. Input: This is the process of entering data and programs in to the computer system. You should know that computer is an electronic machine like any other machine which takes as inputs raw data and performs some processing giving out processed data. Therefore, the input unit takes data from us to the computer in an organized manner for processing.

2. Storage: The process of saving data and instructions permanently is known as storage. Data has to be fed into the system before the actual processing starts. It is because the processing speed of Central Processing Unit (CPU) is so fast that the data has to be provided to CPU with the same speed. Therefore the data is first stored in the storage unit for faster access and processing. This storage unit or the primary storage of the computer system is designed to do the above functionality. It provides space for storing data and instructions.

The storage unit performs the following major functions:

• All data and instructions are stored here before and after processing.

• Intermediate results of processing are also stored here.

3. Processing: The task of performing operations like arithmetic and logical operations is called processing. The Central Processing Unit (CPU) takes data and instructions from the storage unit and makes all sorts of calculations based on the instructions given and the type of data provided. It is then sent back to the storage unit.

4. Output: This is the process of producing results from the data for getting useful information. Similarly the output produced by the computer after processing must also be kept somewhere inside the computer before being given to you in human readable form. Again the output is also stored inside the computer for further processing.

5. Control: The manner how instructions are executed and the above operations are performed. Controlling of all operations like input, processing and output are performed by control unit. It takes care of step by step processing of all operations inside the computer.

FUNCTIONAL UNITS

In order to carry out the operations mentioned in the previous section the computer allocates the task between its various functional units. The computer system is divided into three separate units for its operation. They are

1) arithmetic logical unit

2) control unit.

3) central processing unit.

Arithmetic Logical Unit (ALU) Logical Unit

Logical Unit :After you enter data through the <u>input device</u> it is stored in the primary storage unit. The actual processing of the data and instruction are performed by Arithmetic Logical Unit. The major operations performed by the ALU are addition, subtraction, multiplication, division, logic and comparison. Data is transferred to ALU from storage unit when required. After processing the output is returned back to storage unit for further processing or getting stored.

Control Unit (CU)

The next component of computer is the Control Unit, which acts like the supervisor seeing that things are done in proper fashion. Control Unit is responsible for coordinating various operations using time signal. The control unit determines the sequence in which computer programs and instructions are executed. Things like processing of programs stored in the main <u>memory</u>, interpretation of the instructions and issuing of signals for other units of the computer to execute them. It also acts as a switch board operator when several users access the computer simultaneously. Thereby it coordinates the activities of computer's peripheral equipment as they perform the input and output.

Central Processing Unit (CPU)

The ALU and the CU of a computer system are jointly known as the central processing unit. You may call CPU as the brain of any computer system. It is just like brain that takes all major decisions, makes all sorts of calculations and directs different parts of the computer functions by activating and controlling the operations.

Q3) Describe in detail evolution of internet and its applications.

Ans: The Internet, is a worldwide system of computer networks - a network of networks in which users at any one computer can, if they have permission, get information from any other computer.

The internet links private PCs, public networks and business networks together using telephone lines to form one vast worldwide network The Internet has revolutionized the computer and communications world like nothing before. The invention of the telegraph, telephone, radio, and computer set the stage for this unprecedented integration of capabilities. The Internet is at once a world-wide broadcasting capability, a mechanism for information dissemination, and a medium for collaboration and interaction between individuals and their computers without regard for geographic location.

Applications of internet:

The internet is treated as one of the biggest invention. It has a large number of uses.

1. Communication

2. Job searches

3. Finding books and study material

4. Health and medicine

5. Travel

6. Entertainment

7. Shopping

8. Stock market updates

9. Research

10. Business use of internet: different ways by which intenet can be used for business are:

Services of Internet:

1. Communication:

Email is an important communications service available on the Internet. The concept of sending electronic text messages between parties in a way analogous to mailing letters or memos predates the creation of the Internet. Pictures, documents and other files are sent as email attachments. Emails can be cc-ed to multiple email addresses.

Internet telephony is another common communications service made possible by the creation of the Internet. VoIP stands for Voice-over-Internet Protocol, referring to the protocol that underlies all Internet communication.

2. Data Transfer:

File sharing is an example of transferring large amounts of data across the Internet. A computer file can be emailed to customers, colleagues and friends as an attachment. It can be uploaded to a website or FTP server for easy download by others. Some of the example of file sharing are:-

FTP

TELNET(Remote Computing)

Telnet or remote computing is telecommunication utility software, which uses available telecommunication facility and allows you become a user on a remote computer. Once you gain access to remote computer, you can use it for the intended purpose. The TELNET works in a very step by step procedure. The commands typed on the client computer are sent to the local Internet Service Provider (ISP), and then from the ISP to the remote computer that you have gained access. Most of the ISP provides facility to TELENET into your own account from another city and check your e-mail while you are travelling or away on business.

3. Information:

Many people use the terms Internet and World Wide Web, or just the Web, interchangeably, but the two terms are not synonymous. The World Wide Web is a global set of documents, images and other resources, logically interrelated by hyperlinks and referenced with Uniform Resource Identifiers (URIs). Hypertext Transfer Protocol (HTTP) is the main access protocol of the World Wide Web, but it is only one of the hundreds of communication protocols used on the Internet.

Internet is interconnection of large number of heterogeneous computer networks all over the world that can share information back and forth. These interconnected network exchange information by using same standards and protocols.

Q4) List various symbols used in flowcharts. Draw a flowchart to check whether a number is prime or not.

Ans: A flowchart is a type of diagram that represents an algorithm, workflow or process, showing the steps as boxes of various kinds, and their order by connecting them with arrows. Flowcharts use special shapes to represent different types of actions or steps in a process. Lines and arrows show the sequence of the steps, and the relationships among them. These are known as flowchart symbols. The type of diagram dictates the flowchart symbols that are used.

Shape	Name	Description
⟶	Flow Line	An arrow coming from one symbol and ending at another symbol represents that control passes to the symbol the arrow points to. The line for the arrow can be solid or dashed.
(oval)	Terminal	Represented as circles, ovals, or rounded rectangles. They usually contain the word "Start" or "End"
(rectangle)	Process	Represented as rectangles. This shape is used to show that something is performed. Examples: "Add 1 to X",
(diamond)	Decision	Represented as a diamond (rhombus) showing where a decision is necessary, commonly a Yes/No question or True/False test. The conditional symbol is peculiar in that it has two arrows coming out of it, usually from the bottom point and right point, one corresponding to Yes or True, and one corresponding to No or False.
(parallelogram)	Input/Output	Represented as a parallelogram. Involves receiving data and displaying processed data.

(Check Prime Number) Let N be a Positive Integer. The Number N will be a Prime Number if it is only divisible by 1 and N. If N is divisible by one or more numbers other than 1 and N then it will not be Prime Number. Since a number is always divisible by 1 and itself. Thus in this algorithm N is divided by 2 then 3 then 4 till N – 1. If N is divisible by any number form 2 to N – 1 then is not a Prime Number. Otherwise it is a Prime Number.

Flowchart to check whether a number is prime or not:

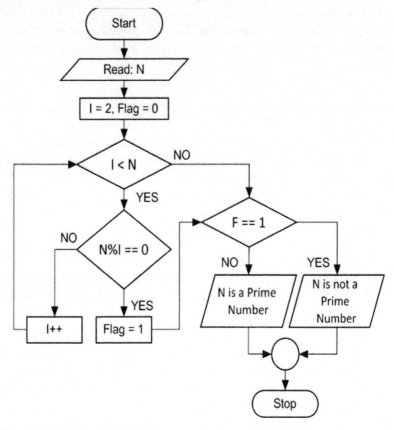

Q5) Describe mail merge feature of a word processing software.

Ans: Mail merge is a feature on word processing application software that enables users to develop personalized letters, greeting cards and other communication with names and addresses stored in a database. It is very easy to proofread a single letter which is then used as the template for many others. In addition, when the template has been created, it can be saved and used again in the future.

Mail Merge is a powerful tool for writing and sending a personalized letter or e-mail to many different people at the same time. User can also use it to create envelopes or labels with each recipient' information. Mail Merge imports data from another source such as Excel and then uses that data to replace placeholders throughout your message with the relevant information for each individual you are messaging. The user can use it to quickly create personalized messages for hundreds of people at once.

The biggest advantage of mail merge is that a company can write and send one standard letter to a large number of stakeholders, such as its shareholders, without manually adding each name and address. Mail merge can generate hundreds of letters and envelopes that are tailored to read as though they were written to individuals.

First, the computer user creates a database of various field names of the desired addressees and then writes the letter linking it to the database. Next, the user employs a query to find a set of people who are targeted to receive a copy of the letter. The mail merge wizard then prompts the user to enter the appropriate details of each addressee. The wizard finalizes the process by taking data from the prepared database and produces a copy of the letter for each person in the database. The only disadvantage is that letters can lack a certain level of personal engagement.

Six Steps to Completing a Mail-Merge

Mail merging means to plug data from an address table into form letters, e-mail messages, envelopes, address labels, or a directory. To start a mail merge, choose Tools | Letters and Mailings | Mail Merge Wizard to open the Mail Merge task pane.

Step 1: Select a Document Type The first step is to select what Word calls a "document type" in the Mail Merge task pane, what kind of mail-merge you want to undertake: form letters, e-mail messages, envelopes for mass-mailings, labels for mass-mailings, or a directory (a list or catalog). Choose an option button and click Next at the bottom of the task pane to go to step 2.

Step 2: Select a Starting Document What Word calls the "starting document" is the document in which the merging takes place. In other words, the address or other data you retrieve will land in the document you choose or create now. You can create a new start document or use an existing one. In the case of labels and envelopes, you tell Word what size labels or envelopes you intend to print on. In the case of form letters, e-mail messages, and directories, you supply the text either by making use of a document you've written already or writing a new document.

Step 3: Select Recipients In step 3, you tell Word where to get the data that you will merge into the starting document you created or supplied in step 2. You can retrieve the data from a table in a Word document, an Access database table or query, or the address book or contact list where you store your addresses. You can also create a new list for the data if you haven't entered the data in a file yet.

Step 4: Write/Arrange Your Document In step 4, you insert the merge fields, the parts of the starting document that differ from recipient to recipient. By inserting merge fields, you tell Word where to plug information from the data source into the starting document. You also tell Word which data to take from the data source. Word offers special tools for entering an address block – the recipient's address, including his or her name, company, title, street address, city, and zip code.

Step 5: Preview Your Document In step 5, you get a chance to see what your form letters, e-mail messages, envelopes, labels, or directory will look like after they are printed or sent. In this step, you find out what the document will look like when real data is plugged into it. If something is amiss in the document, you can click the Previous link to return to step 4, the Write/Arrange your document task pane, and make changes there.

Step 6: Complete the Merge Step 6 is where you complete the merge by either printing a new document or saving the new file and printing it later. By saving the merged data in a new file, you can edit the file before printing it. In the case of e-mail messages, you click the Electronic Mail link to tell Word to send the e-mail messages.

Section C

Q6) What do you mean by iteration? List and explain various constructs for iteration available in C++.

Ans: Iteration is the repetition of a function or process in a computer program. Iterations of functions are common in computer programming, since they allow multiple blocks of data to be processed in sequence..

Iteration, is a process wherein a set of instructions or structures are repeated in a sequence a specified number of times or until a condition is met. When the first set of instructions is executed again, it is called an iteration. When a sequence of instructions is executed in a repeated manner, it is called a loop. This is typically done using a "while loop" or "for loop". These loops will repeat a process until a certain number or case is reached. Recursive functions also use iteration, though instead of repeating a process, the entire function repeats itself.

Computers are very good at performing repetitive tasks very quickly. **Various loops available in C++ are:**

while Loops (Condition-Controlled Loops)

Both while loops and do-while loops are condition-controlled, meaning that they continue to loop until some condition is met.Both while and do-while loops alternate between performing actions and testing for the stopping condition.

While loops check for the stopping condition first, and may not execute the body of the loop at all if the condition is initially false.

Syntax:

> while(condition)
>
>> body;

where the body can be either a single statement or a block of statements .

do-while Loops

do-while loops are like while loops, except that the test is performed at the end of the loop rather than the beginning. The loop will be performed at least once, which is useful for checking user input among other things.

Syntax:

> do {
>
>> body;
>
> } while(condition);

The body can be either a single statement or a block of statements.

for Loops

for-loops are counter-controlled, they are normally used whenever the number of iterations is known in advance.

Syntax:

Details:

The initialization step occurs one time only, before the loop begins.

The condition is tested at the beginning of each iteration of the loop.

If the condition is true, then the body of the loop is executed next.

If the condition is false, then the body is not executed, and execution continues with the code following the loop.

The incrementation happens AFTER the execution of the body, and only when the body is executed.

Q7) With the help of an example, describe passing of strings to a function.

Ans: Array of characters is called a string. A string is terminated by a null character /0.

Strings are declared in a similar manner as arrays. Only difference is that, strings are of char type. Like

     char s[5];

Passing Strings to Functions:

Strings are just char arrays. So, they can be passed to a function in a similar manner as arrays. In order to pass the string to a function, the array name need to be specified in the parameter list. The name of the array should be written in the square brackets, in the parameter list of the function calling statement.

Example:

```
#include <stdio.h>
void displayString(char str[]);
int main()
{
  char str[50];
   printf("Enter string: ");
   gets(str);
   displayString(str);    // Passing string c to function.
   return 0;
}
void displayString(char str[]){
   printf("String Output: ");
   puts(str);
}
```

Here, string c is passed from main() function to user-defined function displayString(). In function declaration, str[] is the formal argument.

Q8) What do you mean by member functions? Describe how member functions can be defined inside a class and outside of a class. What is the difference between these two types of definitions?

Ans: A member function of a class is a function that has its definition or its prototype within the class definition like any other variable. It operates on any object of the class of which it is a member, and has access to all the members of a class for that object.

Member functions are the functions, which have their declaration inside the class definition and works on the data members of the class. The definition of member functions can be inside or outside the definition of class.

If the member function is defined inside the class definition it can be defined directly, but if its defined outside the class, then we have to use the scope resolution :: operator along with class name along with function.

Member functions can be defined in two places:-

Outside the class definition

The member functions of a class can be defied outside the class definitions. It is only declared inside the class but defined outside the class. Defining a member function outside a class requires the function declaration to be provided inside the class definition. The member function is declared inside the class like a normal function. This declaration informs the compiler that the function is a member of the class and that it has been defined outside the class. After a member function is declared inside the class, it must be defined (outside the class) in the program.

The general form of member function definition outside the class definition is:

Return_type Class_name:: function_name (argument list)

{

Function body

}

A program to add two numbers defining a member getdata () and display () inside a class named sum and displaying the result.

Example

#include<iostream.h>

#include<conio.h>

Class sum

{

Int A, B, Total;

Public:

Void getdata ();

Void display ();

};

Void sum:: getdata ()

{

Cout<<" \n enter the value of A and B";

Cin>>A>>B;

}

Void sum:: display ()

{

Total =A+B;

Cout<<"\n the sum of A and B="<<Total;

}

void main ()

{

Sum a;

a.getdata ();

a.display ();

getch ();

}

Inside the class definition

The member function of a class can be declared and defined inside the class definition.

A member function of a class can also be defined inside the class. However, when a member function is defined inside the class, the class name and the scope resolution operator are not specified in the function header. Moreover, the member functions defined inside a class definition are by default inline functions.

Example

```
#include<iostream.h>
#include<conio.h>
Class sum
{
Private:
Int A, B, Total;
Public:
Void getdata ()
{
Cout<,"\n enter the value of A and B";
Cin>>A>>B;
}
Void display ()
{
Total = A+B;
Cout<<"\n the sum of A and B="<<total;
}
};
Void main ()
{
Sum a;
a.getdata ();
a.display ();
getch ();
}
```

Q9) Write a program in C++ to count number of characters in a file.

Ans: A file is an object on a computer that stores data, information, settings, or commands used with a computer program.

Program:

```cpp
#include<iostream.h>
#include<fstream.h>
#include<string.h>
#include<conio.h>
using namespace std;
// start of main program
int main()
{
        string filename;
        cout<<"Please enter the data file name: ";
        // reads the filename from the user
        cin>>filename;
          // open the file for input.
        ifstream infile(filename, std::ifstream::in);
        // create the stream in read-only mode
        if(!infile) {
                cout << "Cannot open file for reading.\n";
                getch();
                    return 1;
        }
      // declares character and integer variables
        char ch,c;
        int count=1;
        int i=0;
        int count1=1;
        // running the loop until file will end
        while(infile.get(ch))
        {
                cout<<ch;
                if(ch==' ')
```

```
        {

                count++;

                count1++;

        }

        else if(ch==' ')

                count1++;

        i=i+1;

    }cout<<"";
```

// display the number of character, words and line

```
    cout<<"\nNumber of characters: "<<i-(count-1+count1-1)<<"";

    cout<<"\nNumber of words: "<<count1<<"";

    cout<<"\nNumber of lines: "<<count<<"";
```

// closes the file

```
    infile.close();

    getch();

    return 0;

}
```

Total No. of Questions : 09

B.Tech.(2011 Onwards) (Sem.-1,2)

FUNDAMENTALS OF COMPUTER PROGRAMMING ANDIN FORMATION TECHNOLOGY

Subject Code:BTCS-101Paper ID : [Al 108]

Time:3Hrs.   Max. Marks:60

INSTRUCTIONS TO CANDIDATES :

1. SECTION-A is COMPULSORY consisting of TEN questions carrying TWO marks each,

2. SECTION - B & C. have FOUR questions each.

3. Attempt any FIVE questions from SECTIONB & C carrying EIGHT marks each.

4. Select at least TWO questions from SECTION

SECTION-A

1.   Write briefly:

a)   What is conditional operator?

1. They are also called as Ternary Operator .

2. They also called as ?: operator

3. Ternary Operators takes on 3 Arguments

Syntax of Ternary Operator:

Expression_1 ? Expression_2 : Expression_3

☐ Expression_1 is Condition

☐ Expression_2 is statement followed if Condition is True

☐ Expression_3 is statement followed if Condition is False.

b)   Differentiate between a++ and ++a?

c)   a++ makes a copy, increases i, and returns the copy (old value).

d)   ++a increases i, and returns i.

In your example it is all about speed. ++i will be the faster than i++ since it doesn't make a copy.

However a compiler will probably optimize it away since you are not storing the returned value from the increment operator in your example, but this is only possible for fundamental types like aint

In Pre-Increment the initial value is first incremented and then used inside the expression.

a=++i;

In this example suppose the value of variable i is 5 then value of variable a will be 6 because, the value of i gets modified before using it in a expression.

In Post-Increment value is first used in a expression and then incremented.

a=i++;

In this example suppose the value of variable i is 5 then value of variable a will be 5 because, value of i gets incremented only after assigning the value 5 to a

c)what are the additional advantages offor loop

For loops are great when you need to iterate a certain number of times. While loops are great when you need to loop until a certain condition becomes false.

For loops must use a comparison like so:

var> 1

They cannot accept Boolean values(true or false).

While loops can accept Boolean values:

!var

Seriously, the advantage of using for_each is that the reader knows that the loop doesn't terminate prematurely. This has to be weighed against the fact the code you execute each pass must be separate---if the code is more or less general, and has a good name, this is an advantage; if the code is specialized to the place making the call, and has no good name, then it is bad.

d)   Differentiate between <<&>> operator?

The bitwise shift operators are the right-shift operator (>>), which moves the bits of `shift_expression` to the right, and the left-shift operator (<<), which moves the bits of `shift_expression` to the left. [1]

Syntax

shift-expression << additive-expression

shift-expression >> additive-expression

e)   What do you mean by the term word wrapping?

In word processing, a feature that causes the word processor to force all text to fit within the defined margins. When you fill one line with text, the word processor automatically jumps to the next line so that you are not required to keep track of line lengths and to press the Return key after each line. The word processor divides lines in such a way that a word is never split between two lines (unless the word processor supports *hyphenation*).

Word wrap also occurs if you change the margins. In this case, the word processor readjusts all the text so that it fits within the new margins.

f)   What is the difference between gutter and mirror margins?

Word includes a unique setting that allows you to "mirror" the margins of a page depending on whether the page is an odd or even page. Mirror margins are typically used to designate a page layout that will eventually be two-sided.ou can set top, bottom, inside (towards the binding) and outside (left and right) margins when you have mirror margins selected. You can also specify a gutter margin, which is the amount of space added to the inside margins to allow for binding of the final book.

If your document won't be printed on both sides of a piece of paper and you are not worried about any particular binding of the final output (including punching holes for use in a binder), then mirror margins won't be of any real value for you; you can safely ignore it. If, however, you will be duplexing your output and you do need to worry about binding, then choose mirror margins and play with your margin settings to get just the output that you need.

g)   What is the application of scope resolution in c++?

1.   It permits a program to reference an identifier in the global scope that has been hidden by another identifier with the same name in the local scope.

2.   It is used to access an item that is outside the current scope.

3.   It is used for distinguishing class members and defining class methods.

4.   A major application of the scope resolution operator is in the classes to identify the class to which a member function belongs.

h)   How does pointer works with two dimensional arrays?

First, we will allocate memory for an array which contains a set of pointers. Next, we will allocate memory for each array which is pointed by the pointers. The deallocation of memory is done in the reverse order of memory allocation.

int **dynamicArray = 0;

//memory allocated for elements of rows.

dynamicArray = newint *[ROWS] ;

//memory allocated for elements of each column.

for(inti = 0 ; i< ROWS ; i++)
dynamicArray[i] = newint[COLUMNS];

//free the allocated memory

```
for( inti = 0 ; i< ROWS ; i++ )

delete [] dynamicArray[i] ;

delete [] dynamicArray ;
```

i)　　　Distinguish between

1) int*ptr=new int(5)

2) int*ptr=new int[5]

It allocates one object of type `int` and initialized it to value `5`.

I)　　　What is the purpose of prototype and scope?

A function prototype is a function declaration that specifies the data types of its arguments in the parameter list. The compiler uses the information in a function prototype to ensure that the corresponding function definition and all corresponding function declarations and calls within the scope of the prototype contain the correct number of arguments or parameters, and that each argument or parameter is of the correct data type.

Prototypes are syntactically distinguished from the old style of function declaration. The two styles can be mixed for any single function, but this is not recommended. The following is a comparison of the old and the prototype styles of declaration:

Old style:

- Functions can be declared implicitly by their appearance in a call.

- Arguments to functions undergo the default conversions before the call.

- The number and type of arguments are not checked.

SECTION-B

2.a)Explain the feature of formatting the paragraph,grouping the images and mail merge tools of MS- word with suitable examples.

paragraph is a unit of text or other content that starts at the beginning of a document, immediately after a hard return (a carriage return), a page break, or a section break, or at the beginning of a table cell, header, footer, or list of footnotes and ends with a hard return (carriage return) or at the end of a table cell. Word documents generally contain paragraphs with different formatting. Even a very simple document with a centered heading and a justified body contains paragraphs with two different types of formatting.

Alignment

Alignment or *justification* refers to the way in which the lines of a paragraph are aligned. There are four types of alignment, and the type of alignment of the paragraph where your cursor is located is indicated by the highlighted button in the **Paragraph** group on the **Home** tab.

• With *left alignment* (≣) (the default), the left-hand ends of all the lines in the paragraph are aligned along the left-hand margin of the text area.

• With *center alignment* (≣), the mid-points (centers) of all the lines in the paragraph are aligned along the same imaginary vertical line at the center of the text area between the margins.

• With *right alignment* (≣), the right-hand ends of all the lines in the paragraph are aligned along the right-hand margin of the text area.

Line spacing refers to the vertical distance between the lines within a paragraph and determines the location of each line relative to the line above it. Line spacing can be specified by name (single, 1.5 lines, double), by a number that indicates a multiple of single spacing (for example, 2.0 is equivalent to double spacing), and by an exact distance in points, where a point (pt) is equal to 1/72 of an inch.

Paragraph Spacing

The spacing between your paragraphs is determined by the *spacing before it* and the *spacing after it* that are set for each paragraph. You can modify the spacing before a paragraph and the spacing after it by changing the values in the applicable boxes in the **Paragraph** group on the **Page Layout** tab.

The Mail Merge Toolkit dialogue looks very similar to the standard Microsoft Office box "Merge to Electronic Mail" (see screenshot). In that box, like in the standard one, you can choose the data field containing recipient addresses, set message subject (btw, in Mail Merge Toolkit you can use automatic data field insertion like in a document text), set the format, and choose files to be attached to each message if necessary.

With Mail Merge Toolkit you can use all the features of Microsoft Office for professional mass mailing! Enjoy the easiest and at the same time most effective work with Mail Merge in Word! Being one of the basic text editors nowadays,

Microsoft Word is applied by the most of PC users. So, Mail Merge in Microsoft Word is of the paramount importance for every Microsoft Office user!

b) What are the various functions of operating system, explain with the example of windows operating system?

Operating System as a Resource Manager

Operating System Also Known as the Resource Manager Means Operating System will Manages all the Resources those are Attached to the System means all the Resource like Memory and <u>Processor</u> and all the Input output Devices those are Attached to the System are Known as the Resources of the <u>Computer</u> System and the Operating system will Manage all the Resources of the System. The Operating System will identify at which Time the <u>CPU</u> will perform which Operation and in which Time the Memory is used by which Programs. And which <u>Input Device</u> will respond to which Request of the user means When the Input and Output Devices are used by the which Programs. So this will manage all the Resources those are attached to the Computer System.

Storage Management

Operating System also Controls the all the Storage Operations means how the data or files will be Stored into the <u>computers</u> and how the Files will be Accessed by the users etc. All the Operations those are Responsible for Storing and Accessing the Files is determined by the Operating System Operating System also Allows us Creation of Files, Creation of Directories and Reading and Writing the data of Files and Directories and also Copy the contents of the Files and the Directories from One Place to Another Place.

1) **Process Management :The Operating System also Treats the Process Management means all the Processes those are given by the user or the Process those are System 's own Process are Handled by the Operating System** . The Operating System will Create the Priorities foe the user and also Start or Stops the Execution of the Process and Also Makes the Child Process after dividing the Large Processes into the Small Processes.

2) **Memory Management:** Operating System also Manages the Memory of the Computer System means Provide the Memory to the Process and Also Deallocate the Memory from the Process. And also defines that if a Process gets completed then this will deallocate the Memory from the Processes.

3) **Extended Machine :** Operating System also behaves like an Extended Machine means Operating system also Provides us Sharing of Files between Multiple Users, also Provides Some Graphical Environments and also Provides

Various Languages for Communications and also Provides Many Complex Operations like using Many Hardware's and Software's.

4) **Mastermind:** Operating System also performs Many Functions and for those Reasons we can say that Operating System is a Mastermind. It provides Booting without an Operating System and Provides Facility to increase the Logical Memory of the Computer System by using the Physical Memory of the Computer System and also provides various Types of Formats Like NTFS and FAT File Systems.

Operating System also controls the Errors those have been Occurred into the Program and Also Provides Recovery of the System when the System gets Damaged Means When due to Some Hardware Failure , if System Doesn't Works properly then this Recover the System and also Correct the System and also Provides us the Backup Facility. And Operating System also breaks the large program into the Smaller Programs those are also called as the threads. And execute those threads one by one.

3. explain nested else if, do while, switch, continue , goto with examples?

Else if

The `if-else` statement allows a choice to be made between two possible alternatives. Sometimes a choice must be made between more than two possibilities. For example the sign function in mathematics returns -1 if the argument is less than zero, returns +1 if the argument is greater than zero and returns zero if the argument is zero. The following C++ statement implements this function:

if (x < 0)

sign = -1;

else

if (x == 0)

sign = 0;

else

sign = 1;

This is an `if-else` statement in which the statement following the `else` is itself an `if-else` statement. If x is less than zero then `sign` is set to -1, however if it is not less than zero the statement following the `else` is executed. In that case if x is equal to zero then `sign` is set to zero and otherwise it is set to 1.

Do while

A **do...while** loop is similar to a while loop, except that a do...while loop is guaranteed to execute at least one time.

Syntax

The syntax of a do...while loop in C++ is:

do {

statement(s);

}while(condition);

Notice that the conditional expression appears at the end of the loop, so the statement(s) in the loop execute once before the condition is tested.

If the condition is true, the flow of control jumps back up to do, and the statement(s) in the loop execute again. This process repeats until the given condition becomes false.

Flow Diagram

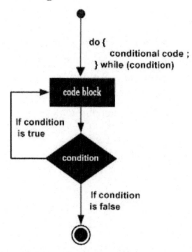

Example

#include<iostream.h>

usingnamespace std;

int main (){

// Local variable declaration:

int a =10;

// do loop execution

do{

cout<<"value of a: "<< a <<endl;

    a = a +1;

}while(a <20);

return0;

The **continue** statement is somewhat the opposite of the **break** statement. It forces the next iteration of the loop to take place, skipping any code in between itself and the test condition of the loop. In **while** and **do-while** loops, a *continue* statement will cause control to go directly to the test condition and then continue the looping process. In the case of the **for** loop, the increment part of the loop continues. One good use of **continue** is to restart a statement sequence when an error occurs.

#include $$$$stdio.h&&&&

main()

{

int x ;

for (x=0 ; x$$$$=100 ; x++) {

if (x%2) continue;

printf(" %d\n" , x);

}

}

4 (a)What are default arguments?why they are used. Explain with example

A **default argument** is an argument to a <u>function</u> that a programmer is not required to specify. In most programming languages, functions may take one or more arguments. Usually, each argument must be specified in full (this is the case in the <u>C programming language</u>[1]). Later languages (for example, in <u>C++</u>) allow the programmer to specify default arguments that always have a value, even if one is not specified when calling the function.

Consider the following function declaration:

intmy_func(inta,intb,intc=12);

This function takes three arguments, of which the last one has a default of twelve. The programmer may call this function in two ways:

result=my_func(1,2,3);

result=my_func(1,2);

In the first case the value for the argument called *c* is specified as normal. In the second case, the argument is omitted, and the default value of *12* will be used instead.

There is no means to know if the argument has been specified by the caller or if the default value was used.

The above-mentioned method is especially useful when one wants to set default criteria so that the function can be called with or without parameters.

Example: Default Argument

```cpp
// C++ Program to demonstrate working of default argument

#include <iostream>
using namespace std;

void display(char = '*', int = 1);

int main()
{
cout<< "No argument passed:\n";
display();

cout<< "\nFirst argument passed:\n";
display('#');

cout<< "\nBoth argument passed:\n";
display('$', 5);

return 0;
}

void display(char c, int n)
{
for(inti = 1; i<= n; ++i)
   {
```

```
cout<< c;
   }
cout<<endl;

}
```

(b) Using pointer notation,write some code that will transfer 80 characters from string S1 to string S2.

C strings

In standard C strings are created as *arrays of char*.

A **null** character (ASCII 0) in the array signals the effective end of the array of char; that is, it marks the end of the string. Characters in the array beyond the **null** are ignored by the functions designed to work on these strings.

A set of standard string manipulation functions are provided in the interface defined in <string.h>.

Since a string is an array of char, you can manipulate it with array notation (subscripts).

However, it is often easier to use the string functions - which mostly use *pointer* notation rather than array notation.

We will look at both approaches.

So how to you create a string?

1. Define an array of char.

char s[80];

Note that we hereby reserve 80 bytes of memory for this string. We are not obligated to use it all, but we better not overfill it or we will be in trouble (because we would overwrite memory after it).

2. Put some chars in it and end it with a null. For now, let's look at the string as an array. So we could do this:

s[0] = 'J';   // J as a char

s[1] = 'i';

s[2] = 'm';

s[3] = 0;

Note that because chars and ints are interchangeable in C, we can assign the integer 0 to s[3]. That is the null character.

However, we **cannot do this** to insert the null char:

s[3] = '0'; // Char '0' is ASCII 48, not ASCII 0

There is one other common way to represent the null character:

s[3] = '\0'; // backslash-zero

This emphasizes the fact that it is a char.

So we have an 80-byte array, and we use only the first 4 bytes.

However, we can now print it using *cout*:

cout<< s; // prints: Jim

If we had forgotten to put in the terminating null, this *cout* could print something like:

Jim. %x6^^* #8, ,d @ b,,......

That is, it would print bytes in memory starting at s, interpreted as chars, until it found (by chance) a null (zero-valued byte).

There are simpler ways to initialize a string:

1. Based on the fact that a string is an array of char, we can do the following:

char s[80] = {'J', 'i', 'm', '\0'}; // here we must use '\0'

in this case, the rest of the array would contain all 0's.

2. There is a shortcut that is allowed by C:

char s[80] = "Jim";

in this case also, the rest of the array would contain all 0's.

3. Looking ahead, there is a string function that will copy one string value into another:

char s[80];

...

strcpy(s, "Jim");

in this case, the rest of the array (after the terminating null) would contain whatever was there before the *strcpy()*.

Since a string is an array of chars, we can look at individual chars in the string using array notation.

cout<< s[2]; // displays: m

Suppose we want a function that will return the Ith character of a string. We could write it as follows:

charIthChar(char s[], inti)

```
{
return s[i];
}
```

And we could call it as:

cout<<IthChar(s, 2));   // displays: m

Note how we designed the function:

- it returns a char
- it takes 2 arguments:
  - o   an array of char (the string)
  - o   the subscript of the char desired

Note also what would happen if we used:

charch;

ch = IthChar(s, 10); // or

ch = IthChar(s, j);   // if j has a value > 3

It would return some random byte (char) that happened to be in memory at 10 bytes (or j bytes) beyond s - at s[10] or s[j]. But the actual effective string is just "Jim". So we don't know what is in s[10] or s[j]. And so we don't know what it would be.

We could find out, of course, if we *cout*-ed the character returned, but it would be meaningless. It was never assigned a value, so its value is random.

One way to fix the function so we couldn't make this mistake is to re-design the function to **return** a code (0 = fail, 1 = ok, for example), and to **pass back** the char (if found). We need to know if the subscript *i* is beyond the end of the string (the null).

intIthChar(char s[], inti, char *ch)

```
{
int p;
```

```
for (p = 0; p <= i; p++)
    // if null is before ithpos in s, return(fail)
if (s[p] == '\0')
return 0;

    // if we're here, we got to ith char
    // without encountering '\0'
    *ch = s[i];
return 1;
    }
```

This considers *s* simply as an array of char, recognizes that the 0 terminates the effective string, and makes use of array notation to do all this.

We could (again, looking ahead) use one of the standard C string functions to help. In particular, there's a function called *strlen()* that can help:

```
intIthChar(char s[], inti, int *ch)

    {
if (i>strlen(s)-1)// ?? check this carefully
return 0;                  // fail

    *ch = s[i];            // pass back ith char
    return 1;              // success
    }
```

Let's check the if-condition carefully. Suppose s has the string "dog"

subscript: 0 1 2 3 4

string: d o g 0 ? ? etc.

strlen(s) is 3 so we want this condition to be true if i is 3 or more (and then return 0). Another way to say it is that we want the condition to be false if i is 0, or 1, or 2, but not if it's more than that (so that we can go on and pass back one of the chars in the string).

So if (i> 2) - for this example - we want the condition to be true so that we will execute the return(0).. Since *strlen(s)* is 3, we can code *strlen(s) - 1* to represent 2.

Alternately (verify this yourself) we could use >= *strlen(s)*.

b) Write a program to palindrome a string by using pointer.

```
1.    #include<stdio.h>
2.    #include<conio.h>
3.    void main(){
4.          char*a;
5.          inti,len,flag=0;
6.          clrscr();
7.          printf("\nENTER A STRING: ");
8.          gets(a);
9.          len=strlen(a);
10.         for(i=0;i<len;i++){
11.                 if(a[i]==a[len-i-1])
12.                       flag=flag+1;
13.         }
14.         if(flag==len)
15.         printf("\nTHE STRING IS PALINDROM");else
16.         printf("\nTHE STRING IS NOT PALINDROM");
17.         getch();
18.    }
```

7) (a) Differentiate betlveen physical data organization and logical data organization

Logical and physical database models are required in order to visually present the database that has been proposed for a certain business requirement. The models help in showing the association of business requirements and the database objects. This is necessary in order to gather all requirements of the database accurately and completely. Data modeling is the link between the system requirements and business needs. There are two data models, logical and physical.

Logical Database Model

Logical database modeling is required for compiling business requirements and representing the requirements as a model. It is mainly associated with the gathering of business needs rather than the database design. The information that needs to be gathered is about organizational units, business entities, and business processes.

Once the information is compiled, reports and diagrams are made, including these:

ERD–Entity relationship diagram shows the relationship between different categories of data and shows the different categories of data required for the development of a database.

Business process diagram–It shows the activities of individuals within the company. It shows how the data moves within the organization based on which application interface can be designed.

Feedback documentation by users.

Logical database models basically determine if all the requirements of the business have been gathered. It is reviewed by developers, management, and finally the end users to see if more information needs to be gathered before physical modeling starts.

Physical Database Model

Physical database modeling deals with designing the actual database based on the requirements gathered during logical database modeling. All the information gathered is converted into relational models and business models. During physical modeling, objects are defined at a level called a schema level. A schema is considered a group of objects which are related to each other in a database. Tables and columns are made according to the information provided during logical modeling. Primary keys, unique keys, and foreign keys are defined in order to provide constraints. Indexes and snapshots are defined. Data can be summarized, and users are provided with an alternative perspective once the tables have been created.

(b) write a c++ program which reads input from a File DING.cpp to count number of characters and words of the file.

```
#include<iostream.h>
#include<fstream.h>


int main()
{
ifstream fin("Ding.txt"); //opening text file
int line=1,word=1,size; //will not count first word and last line so initial value is
1
charch;
fin.seekg(0,ios::end); //bring file pointer position to end of file
size=fin.tellg(); //count number of bytes till current postion for file pointer
fin.seekg(0,ios::beg); //bring position of file pointer to begining of file
```

```
while(fin)
{
  fin.get(ch);
  if(ch==' '||ch=='n')
   word++;

  if(ch=='n')
   line++;
}
cout<<"Lines="<<line<<"nWords="<<word<<"nSize="<<size<<"n";
fin.close(); //closing file
return 0;
}
```

8. write a c++ program to illustrate the concept of abstract crass & pure virtual function.

Abstract Class

Abstract Class is a class which contains atleast one Pure Virtual function in it. Abstract classes are used to provide an Interface for its sub classes. Classes inheriting an Abstract Class must provide definition to the pure virtual function, otherwise they will also become abstract class.

Characteristics of Abstract Class

1. Abstract class cannot be instantiated, but pointers and refrences of Abstract class type can be created.

2. Abstract class can have normal functions and variables along with a pure virtual function.

3. Abstract classes are mainly used for Upcasting, so that its derived classes can use its interface.

4. Classes inheriting an Abstract Class must implement all pure virtual functions, or else they will become Abstract too.

Pure Virtual Functions

Pure virtual Functions are virtual functions with no definition. They start with **virtual** keyword and ends with = 0. Here is the syntax for a pure virtual function,

virtual void f() = 0;

Example of Abstract Class

```
class Base       //Abstract base class
{
public:
virtual void show() = 0;      //Pure Virtual Function
};

classDerived:public Base
{
public:
voidshow()
{ cout<< "Implementation of Virtual Function in Derived class"; }
};

int main()
{
Base obj;      //Compile Time Error
Base *b;
Derived d;
b = &d;
b->show();
}
```

9) (a) Is constructor overloading different from ordinary function overloading ?How can you overload a destructor?

Constructor Overloading

Just like other member functions, constructors can also be overloaded. Infact when you have both default and parameterized constructors defined in your class you are having Overloaded Constructors, one with no parameter and other with parameter.

You can have any number of Constructors in a class that differ in parameter list.

class Student

```
{
introllno;
string name;
public:
Student(int x)
{
rollno=x;
name="None";
}
Student(int x, string str)
{
rollno=x ;
name=str ;
}
};

int main()
{
Student A(10);
Student B(11,"Ram");
}
```

In above case we have defined two constructors with different parameters, hence overloading the constructors.

One more important thing, if you define any constructor explicitly, then the compiler will not provide default constructor and you will have to define it yourself.

In the above case if we write Student S; in **main()**, it will lead to a compile time error, because we haven't defined default constructor, and compiler will not provide its default constructor because we have defined other parameterized constructors.

Destructors

Destructor is a special class function which destroys the object as soon as the scope of object ends. The destructor is called automatically by the compiler when the object goes out of scope.

The syntax for destructor is same as that for the constructor, the class name is used for the name of destructor, with a **tilde~** sign as prefix to it.

```
class A
{
public:
~A();
};
```

Destructors will never have any arguments.

(b) Write a C++ program to overload a constructor. Take your ownassumptions.

Constructors

Constructors are special class functions which performs initialization of every object. The Compiler calls the Constructor whenever an object is created. Constructorsiitialize values to object members after storage is allocated to the object.

```
class A
{
int x;
public:
A(); //Constructor
};
```

While defining a contructor you must remeber that the name of constructor will be same as the name of the class, and contructors never have return type.

Constructors can be defined either inside the class definition or outside class definition using class name and scope resolution **: :** operator.

```
class A
{
inti;
public:
A(); //Constructor declared
};

A::A()  // Constructor definition
{
i=1;
}
```

Types of Constructors

Constructors are of three types :
1.   Default Constructor
2.   Parametrized Constructor
3.   Copy COnstructor

Default Constructor

Default constructor is the constructor which doesn't take any argument. It has no parameter.

Syntax :
class_name ()
{ Constructor Definition }
Example :
class Cube
{
int side;
public:
Cube()
 {
side=10;
 }
};

int main()
{
Cube c;
cout<<c.side;
}
Output : 10

In this case, as soon as the object is created the constructor is called which initializes its data members.

A default constructor is so important for initialization of object members, that even if we do not define a constructor explicitly, the compiler will provide a default constructor implicitly.

class Cube
{
int side;

```
};

int main()
{
 Cube c;
cout<<c.side;
}
```
Output : 0

In this case, default constructor provided by the compiler will be called which will initialize the object data members to default value, that will be 0 in this case.

Parameterized Constructor

These are the constructors with parameter. Using this Constructor you can provide different values to data members of different objects, by passing the appropriate values as argument.

Example :

```
class Cube
{
int side;
public:
Cube(int x)
  {
side=x;
  }
};

int main()
{
 Cube c1(10);
 Cube c2(20);
 Cube c3(30);
cout<< c1.side;
cout<< c2.side;
cout<< c3.side;
}
```
OUTPUT : 10 20 30

By using parameterized construcor in above case, we have initialized 3 objects with user defined values. We can have any number of parameters in a constructor.

Copy Constructor

These are special type of Constructors which takes an object as argument, and is used to copy values of data members of one object into other object. We will study copy constructors in detail later.

Constructor Overloading

Just like other member functions, constructors can also be overloaded. Infact when you have both default and parameterized constructors defined in your class you are having Overloaded Constructors, one with no parameter and other with parameter.

You can have any number of Constructors in a class that differ in parameter list.

```cpp
class Student
{
introllno;
string name;
public:
Student(int x)
 {
rollno=x;
name="None";
 }
Student(int x, string str)
 {
rollno=x ;
name=str ;
 }
};

int main()
{
 Student A(10);
 Student B(11,"Ram");
}
```

In above case we have defined two constructors with different parameters, hence overloading the constructors.

One more important thing, if you define any constructor explicitly, then the compiler will not provide default constructor and you will have to define it yourself.

In the above case if we write `Student S;` in **main**(), it will lead to a compile time error, because we haven't defined default constructor, and compiler will not provide its default constructor because we have defined other parameterized constructors.

EXAMINATION DEC-2014
FUNDAMENTALS OF COMPUTER PROGRAMMING & IT
BTCS-101 PAPER ID-A1108

2. Give short answer of the following:

a. What are the salient features of GUI based O.S.

A **graphical user interface** contains six important **features**, including a pointer, pointing device, icons, desktop, windows and menus. A **GUI** denotes a collection of computer programs that utilize a computer's graphics capabilities to make programs easier to use.

b. What are spreadsheets?

Alternatively referred to as a **worksheet**, a **spreadsheet** is a file made of rows and columns that help sort data, arrange data easily, and calculate numerical data. What makes a spreadsheet software program unique is its ability to calculate values using mathematical formulas and the data in cells.

c. Differenciate between primary memory and secondary memory.

Primary memory is the internal working memory of a computer, and it includes RAM and the cache. Secondary storage is also called external memory, and it includes the computer's hard drive.

d. What are keywords?

In C++, keywords are reserved identifiers which cannot be used as names for the variables in a program.eg. main,if,else,int,void,switch,while etc.. Keywords cannot be used for the –Declaring Variable Name, Declaring Class Name, Declaring Function Name, Declaring Object Name

e. What are operators? Name the operator in c++ to allocate a chunk of memory.

An operator is a symbol which helps the user to command the <u>computer</u> to do a certain mathematical or logical manipulations. Operators are used in C++ language program to operate on data and variables. You can allocate memory at run time within the heap for the variable of a given type using a special operator in C++ which returns the address of the space allocated. This operator is called **new** operator.

There is following generic syntax to use **new** operator to allocate memory dynamically for any data-type.

new data-type;

f.   What do you mean by if-else ladder ?

In C++ programming language the else if ladder is a way of putting multiple ifs together when multipath decisions are involved. It is a one of the types of decision making and branching statements. A multipath decision is a chain of if's in which the statement associated with each else is an if. The general form of else if ladder is as follows –

```
if ( condition 1)
{
     statement - 1;
}
else if (condtion 2)
   {
   statement - 2;
}
  else if ( condition n)
  {
     statement - n;
  }
  else
  {
     default statment;
  }
statement-x;
```

g.   What is recursion? What is its advantage.

Recursion is a programming technique that allows a function to calls itself. A useful way to think of **recursive** functions is to imagine them as a process being performed where one of the instructions is to "repeat the process".

Advantages of recursive functions: - Reduce unnecessary calling of function.Through Recursion one can Solve problems in easy way while its iterative solution is very big and complex.

h.   What do you mean by polymorphism?

The word **polymorphism means** having many forms. Typically, **polymorphism** occurs when there is a hierarchy of classes and they are related by inheritance. **C++ polymorphism means** that a call to a member function will cause a different function to be executed depending on the type of object that invokes the function.

Types of Polymorphism:

C++ provides two different types of polymorphism.

- run-time

- compile-time

i.   What are the different ways to initialize string variable?

Whenever we declare a String then it will contain garbage values inside it. We have to initialize String or Character array before using it. Process of assigning some legal default data to String is Called **Initialization of String**. There are different ways of initializing String in C Programming –

1.   Initializing Unsized Array of Character

2.   Initializing String Directly

3.   Initializing String Using Character Pointer

j.   What is the role of strcmp function.

strcmp function. (String Compare) In the c++ programming language, the **strcmp function** returns a negative, zero, or positive integer depending on whether the object pointed to by s1 is less than, equal to, or greater than the object pointed to by s2.

PART-A

3.   Explain the working of computer system and its associated peripherals.

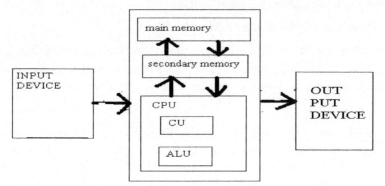

BLOCK DIAGRAM OF A DIGITAL COMPUTER

A **computer peripheral** is a device that is connected to a computer .

Types of Peripheral Devices

There are many different peripheral devices, but they fall into three general categories:

1.   **Input devices**, such as a mouse and a keyboard

2.   **Output devices**, such as a monitor and a printer

3.   **Storage devices**, such as a hard drive or flash drive

Some devices fall into more than one category. Consider a CD-ROM drive; you can use it to read data or music (input), and you can use it to write data to a CD (output).

Peripheral devices can be **external** or **internal**. For example, a printer is an external device that you connect using a cable, while an optical disc drive is typically located inside the computer case. Internal peripheral devices are also referred to as integrated peripherals. When most people refer to peripherals, they typically mean external ones.

The concept of what exactly is 'peripheral' is therefore somewhat fluid. For a desktop computer, a keyboard and a monitor are considered peripherals - you can easily connect and disconnect them and replace them if needed. For a laptop computer, these components are built into the computer system and can't be easily removed.

The term 'peripheral' also does not mean it is not essential for the function of the computer. Some devices, such as a printer, can be disconnected and the computer will keep on working just fine. However, remove the monitor of a desktop computer and it becomes pretty much useless.

4.   What is operating system? List its functions.

An **operating system (OS)** is the program that, after being initially loaded into the **computer** by a boot program, manages all the other programs in a **computer**. The other programs are called applications or application programs.

Its functions:

Resource Manager :operating System Also Known as the Resource Manager Means Operating System will Manages all the Resources those are Attached to the System means all the Resource like Memory and Processor and all the Input output Devices those are Attached to the System are Known as the Resources of the Computer System and the Operating system will Manage all the Resources of the System. The Operating System will identify at which Time the CPU will perform which Operation and in which Time the Memory is used by which Programs. And which Input Device will respond to which Request of the user means When the Input and Output Devices are used by the which Programs. So this will manage all the Resources those are attached to the Computer System.

Storage Management: Operating System also Controls the all the Storage Operations means how the data or files will be Stored into the computers and how the Files will be Accessed by the users etc. All the Operations those are Responsible for Storing and Accessing the Files is determined by the Operating System Operating System also Allows us Creation of Files, Creation of Directories and Reading and Writing the data of Files and Directories and also Copy the contents of the Files and the Directories from One Place to Another Place.

Process Management : The Operating System also Treats the Process Management means all the Processes those are given by the user or the Process those are System 's own Process are Handled by the Operating System . The Operating System will Create the Priorities foe the user and also Start or Stops the Execution of the Process and Also Makes the Child Process after dividing the Large Processes into the Small Processes.

Memory Management: Operating System also Manages the Memory of the Computer System means Provide the Memory to the Process and Also Deallocate the Memory from the Process. And also defines that if a Process gets completed then this will deallocate the Memory from the Processes.

5.   Define an algorithm. Write an algorithm to check whether a given no. is odd or not.

In programming, algorithm is the set of well defined instruction in sequence to solve a program. An algorithm should always have a clear stopping point.

Qualities of a good algorithm

5.   Inputs and outputs should be defined precisely.

6.   Each step in algorithm should be clear and unambiguous.

7.   Algorithm should be most effective among many different ways to solve a problem.

8.   An algorithm shouldn't have computer code. Instead, the algorithm should be written in such a way that, it can be used in similar programming languages.

An algorithm to check whether a number entered by user is odd or not.

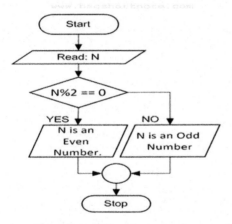

9.   Describe various features that can be used while creating a power point presentation.

PowerPoint is a complete presentation graphics package. It gives you everything you need to produce a professional-looking presentation. **PowerPoint** offers word processing, outlining, drawing, graphing, and presentation management tools- all designed to be easy to use and learn.

To insert a new slide:

Click the New Slide command in the Slides group on the Home tab. A menu will appear with your slide layout options.

To change the layout of an existing slide:

• Select the slide you want to change.

• Click the **Layout** command in the **Slides** group on the Home tab. A menu appears with your options.

To copy and paste a slide:

• Select the slide you want to copy.

• Click the **Copy** command on the Home tab.

• Click inside the **Slides** tab on the left task pane. A **horizontal insertion point** will appear.

• Move the insertion point to the location where you want the copy of the slide to appear.

• Click the **Paste** command on the Home tab. The copied slide will appear.

To delete a slide:

• Select the slide you want to **delete**.

• Click the **Delete** command in the Slides group on the Home tab.

Saving your presentation:

If you are saving a document for the first time, you will need to use the **Save As** command; however, if you have already saved a presentation, you can use the **Save** command.

Insert tables and charts:

Tables and charts are important elements of many slide presentations, and PowerPoint 2007 makes it easier to create and edit them. It's simpler to cut and paste information from Excel spreadsheets, and adding a table or chart to a slide is a point-and-click operation that's done from the Insert tab.

Save as PDF or XPS:

Now you can save PowerPoint presentations as PDF or XPS files.

Secure your presentation:

• We can add digital signatures to the PowerPoint file to authenticate the identity of its creator and to verify that the content hasn't been changed since it was signed.

• You can encrypt the presentation.

PART-B

10.   What are type modifiers? List various type modifiers available in c++.

C++ allows the **char, int,** and **double** data types to have modifiers preceding them. A modifier is used to alter the meaning of the base type so that it more precisely fits the needs of various situations.

The data type modifiers are listed here:

*   signed
*   unsigned
*   long
*   short

The modifiers **signed, unsigned, long,** and **short** can be applied to integer base types. In addition, **signed** and **unsigned** can be applied to char, and **long** can be applied to double. The modifiers **signed** and **unsigned** can also be used as prefix to **long** or **short** modifiers. For example, **unsigned long int**. C++ allows a shorthand notation for declaring **unsigned, short,** or **long** integers. You can simply use the word **unsigned, short,** or **long**, without the int.

Integer Type Modifiers:

By using different number of bytes to store values, C++ offers three types of integers : short, int, and long that can represent up to three different integer sizes. Each comes in both signed and unsigned versions. That gives you a choice of six different integer types. A short integer is at least two bytes. An int integer is at least as big as short. A long is at least four bytes and at least as big as int.

The prefix unsigned makes the integer type not to hold negative values. For instance, if short (2-byte long) represents the range -32768 to +32767, then the unsigned version can represent the range 0 to 65535. This has the advantage of increasing the largest value the variables can hold. Unsigned type are used for quantities that are never negative such as populations, sports scores, inventory counts etc.

The following table summarizes different integer types, their sizes and minimal range they can hold :

Type	Approximate Size (in byte)	Minimal Range
short	2	-32768 to 32767
unsigned short	2	0 to 65,535
signed short	2	same as short
int	2	-32768 to 32767
unsigned int	2	0 to 65,535
signed int	2	same as int
long	4	-2,147,483,648 to 2,147,483,647
unsigned long	4	0 to 4,294,967,295
signed long	4	same as long

Character Type Modifiers:

The char type is really another integer type (as inside memory it actually holds numbers i.e., equivalent codes of characters/symbols). It is guaranteed to be large enough to represent the entire range of basic symbols - all the letters, digits, punctuation and the like - for the target computer system. A single byte can represent the whole range of 256 known characters. The char type can also be signed or unsigned. Unlike int, char is neither signed nor unsigned by default. The choice is left to the C++ implementation in order to allow the implementer to best fit the type to the hardware properties. However, these distinctions are particularly important if you are using char as a numeric type. The unsigned char represents the range 0 to 256 and signed char represents the range -128 to 127.

Type	Approximate Size (in bytes)	Minimal Range
char	1	-128 to 127
unsigned char	1	0 to 255
signed char	1	same as char

The following table summarizes the character types and their minimal ranges :

Floating-point Type Modifiers

C++ has three floating-point types: float, double and long double.These types are described in terms of the number of significant features they can represent and the minimum allowable range of exponents. The type float occupies 4 bytes of memory. Type double occupies 8 bytes, twice as much memory as type float and stores floating-point numbers with much larger range and precision. Floating-point type long double occupies 10 bytes and has only slightly greater range and precision than type double.

Following table summarises floating-point types and the minimal range of values they can hold :

Type	Approximate Size (in bytes)	Minimal Range	Digits of Precision
float	4	3.4×10^{-38} to 3.4×10^{38} - 1	7
double	8	1.7×10^{-308} to 1.7×10^{308} - 1	15
long double	10	3.4×10^{-4932} to 3.4×10^{4932} - 1	19

11.   Describe with the help of example various decision making statements available in c++.

Decision making is about deciding the order of execution of statements based on certain conditions or repeat a group of statements until certain specified conditions are met. C++ handles decision-making by supporting the following statements,

*   *if* statement

*   *switch* statement

Decision making with if statement

The if statement may be implemented in different forms depending on the complexity of conditions to be tested. The different forms are,

1.   Simple if statement

2.   If....else statement

3.   Nested if....else statement

4.   else if statement

Simple if statement

The general form of a simple *if* statement is,

```
if( expression )
{
 statement-inside;
}
 statement-outside;
```

If the *expression* is true, then 'statement-inside' it will be executed, otherwise 'statement-inside' is skipped and only 'statement-outside' is executed.

Example :

```
#include< iostream.h>
int main( )
{
 int x,y;
 x=15;
 y=13;
 if (x > y )
 {
  cout << "x is greater than y";
 }
}
Output :
x is greater than y
```

if...else *statement*

The general form of a simple *if...else* statement is,

```
if( expression )
{
 statement-block1;
}
else
{
 statement-block2;
}
```

If the 'expression' is true, the 'statement-block1' is executed, else 'statement-block1' is skipped and 'statement-block2' is executed.

Example :

```cpp
void main( )
{
int x,y;
x=15;
y=18;
if (x > y )
{
 cout << "x is greater than y";
}
else
{
 cout << "y is greater than x";
}
}
```

Output :

y is greater than x

Nested if....else *statement*

The general form of a nested *if...else* statement is,

```cpp
if( expression )
{
 if( expression1 )
  {
   statement-block1;
  }
 else
  {
   statement-block2;
  }
}
else
{
statement-block3;
}
```

if 'expression' is false the 'statement-block3' will be executed, otherwise it continues to perform the test for 'expression 1' . If the 'expression 1' is true the 'statement-block1' is executed otherwise 'statement-block2' is executed.

Example :

```
void main( )
{
int a,b,c;
clrscr();
cout << "enter 3 number";
cin >> a >> b >> c;
if(a > b)
{
 if( a > c)
 {
  cout << "a is greatest";
 }
 else
 {
  cout << "c is greatest";
 }
}
else
{
 if( b> c)
 {
  cout << "b is greatest";
 }
 else
 {
  printf("c is greatest");
 }
}
getch();
}
```

else-if *ladder*
The general form of else-if ladder is,

```
if(expression 1)
{
statement-block1;
}
else if(expression 2)
{
statement-block2;
}
else if(expression 3 )
{
statement-block3;
}
else
default-statement;
```

The expression is tested from the top(of the ladder) downwards. As soon as the true condition is found, the statement associated with it is executed.

Switch Statement: The if/else statement provides only two variants of actions. But often there are situations that we have to make decisions not only on true/false statements. For this purpose we can use switch statement:

```
switch (expression)
{
case constant1:
  group-of-statements-1;
  break;
case constant2:
  group-of-statements-2;
  break;
  .
  .
  .
default:
  default-group-of-statements
}
```

Switch statement evaluates the expression. If expression is equal to constant1, the group-of-statements-1 is performed, if expression is equal to constant2, the group-of-statements-2; is performed etc. If the expression is not equal to all the case constants – the default-group-of-statements is executed.

12.   What are the different forms of inheritance supported by c++? Explain them with example.

Inheritance in Object Oriented Programming can be described as a process of creating new classes from existing classes. New classes **inherit** some of the properties and behavior of the existing classes. An existing class that is "parent" of a new class is called a base class. ... **Inheritance** is a technique of code reuse.

Types of Inheritance

- Single Inheritance.

- Multiple Inheritance.

- Hierarchical Inheritance.

- Multilevel Inheritance.

- Hybrid Inheritance (also known as Virtual Inheritance)

Single Inheritance

In this type of inheritance one derived class inherits from only one base class. It is the most simplest form of Inheritance.

Multiple Inheritance

In this type of inheritance a single derived class may inherit from two or more than two base classes.

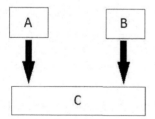

Hierarchical Inheritance

In this type of inheritance, multiple derived classes inherits from a single base class.

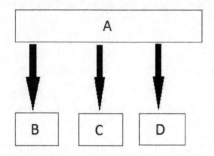

Multilevel Inheritance

In this type of inheritance the derived class inherits from a class, which in turn inherits from some other class. The Super class for one, is sub class for the other.

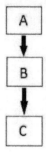

Hybrid (Virtual) Inheritance

Hybrid Inheritance is combination of Hierarchical and Multilevel Inheritance.

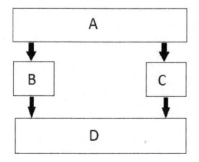

13.   a. What are default arguments? Why are they used?

A default argument is a value provided in function declaration that is automatically assigned by the compiler if caller of the function doesn't provide a value for theargument with default value. Following is a simple C++ example to demonstrate use of default arguments.

Their use:

In C++ programming, you can provide default values for function parameters. The idea behind default argument is simple. If a function is called by passing argument/s, thosearguments are used by the function. But if the argument/s are not passed while invoking a function then, the defaultvalues are used.

b.   Can we have more than one constructor in a class? If yes, explain the need of such situation.

Yes, a class in C++ can have more than one constructor with the same name. this interesting feature of the constructor is known as constructor overloading. All the constructors have the same name as the corresponding class but differ only in terms of their signature (in terms of the number of arguments, or data types of their arguments, or both) as shown in the below program.

```
#include<iostream.h>
Class Account
{
Private :
Int acc_no;
Float balance ;
Public :
Account ( )
```

Appendix: I

C++ built-in Header Files				
alloc.h	dos.h	limits.h	share.h	sys\stat.h
assert.h	errno.h	locale.h	signal.h	sys\timeb.h
bcd.h	fcntl.h	malloc.h	stdarg.h	sys\types.h
bios.h	float.h	math.h	stddef.h	time.h
complex.h	fstream.h	mem.h	stdio.h	utime.h
conio.h	generic.h	memory.h	stdiostr.h	values.h
ctype.h	graphics.h	new.h	stream.h	varargs.h
dir.h	io.h	process.h	string.h	sys\stat.h
direct.h	iomanip.h	search.h	strstrea.h	sys\timeb.h
dirent.h	iostream.h	setjmp.h	sys\locking.h	sys\types.h

List of best and free C/C++ compilers and IDEs for Programmers			
Eclipse	Dev C++	GCC	CC65
NetBeans	CodeLite	Xcode	LCC
Code::Blocks	MinGW	Tiny C – Compiler	SDCC
Digital Mars:	Ultimate++	Portable C Compiler	nesC
C Free	Mirosoft Visual Studio Express	Failsafe C	CC386
Sky IDE	Open Watcom	Pelles C	SubC
Turbo C++	TC	TurboC3	

Turbo C++ Keyboard Shortcuts					
Shortcuts keys	Action	Shortcuts keys	Action	Shortcuts keys	Action
F1	For Help	Alt+X	Quit	Ctrl+F9	Run
F2	Save	Alt+Bksp	Undo	Ctrl+F2	Program reset
F3	Open	Shift+Alt+Bksp	Redo	Alt+F9	Compile
F4	Go to cursor	Shift+Del	Cut	Alt+F4	Inspect
F5	Zoom	Ctrl+Ins	Copy	Ctrl+F4	Evaluate/Modify
F6	Next	Shift+Ins	Paste	Ctrl+F3	Call stack
F7	Trace into	Ctrl+Del	Clear	Ctrl+F8	Toggle breakpoint
F8	Step over	Ctrl+L	Search again	Ctrl+F5	Size/Move
F9	Make	Alt+F7	Previous error	Alt+F3	Close
F10	Menu	Alt+F8	Next error	Alt+F5	User screen
Alt+0	List all	Shift+F1	Index	Ctrl+F7	Add watchb
Ctrl+F1	Topic search	Alt+F1	Previous topic		

Data Types available in C++:

1. Primary(Built-in) Data Types:

    o   character

    o   integer

    o   floating point

    o   boolean

    o   double floating point

    o   void

    o   wide character

2. User Defined Data Types:

    o   Structure

    o   Union

    o   Class

    o   Enumeration

3. Derived Data Types:

    o   Array

    o   Function

    o   Pointer

    o   Reference

The lists of modifiers used in C++ are:

*   signed

*   unsigned

*   long

*   short

Data Type (Keywords)	Description	Size	Typical Range
char	Any single character. It may include a letter, a digit, a punctuation mark, or a space.	1 byte	-128 to 127 or 0 to 255
signed char	Signed character.	1 byte	-128 to 127
unsigned char	Unsigned character.	1 byte	0 to 255
wchar_t	Wide character.	2 or 4 bytes	1 wide character
Data Type (Keywords)	Description	Size	Typical Range
int	Integer.	4 bytes	-2147483648 to 2147483647
signed int	Signed integer. Values may be negative, positive, or zero.	4 bytes	-2147483648 to 2147483647
unsigned int	Unsigned integer. Values are always positive or zero. Never negative.	4 bytes	0 to 4294967295
short	Short integer.	2 bytes	-32768 to 32767
signed short	Signed short integer. Values may be negative, positive, or zero.	2 bytes	-32768 to 32767
unsigned short	Unsigned short integer. Values are always positive or zero. Never negative.	2 bytes	0 to 65535
long	Long integer.	4 bytes	-2147483648 to 2147483647
signed long	Signed long integer. Values may be negative, positive, or zero.	4 bytes	-2147483648 to 2147483647

| unsigned long | Unsigned long integer. Values are always positive or zero. Never negative. | 4 bytes | 0 to 4294967295 |

Floating-point Data Types

Data Type (Keywords)	Description	Size	Typical Range
float	Floating point number. There is no fixed number of digits before or after the decimal point.	4 bytes	+/- 3.4e +/- 38 (~7 digits)
double	Double precision floating point number. More accurate compared to float.	8 bytes	+/- 1.7e +/- 308 (~15 digits)
long double	Long double precision floating point number.	8 bytes	+/- 1.7e +/- 308 (~15 digits)

Boolean Data Type

Data Type (Keywords)	Description	Size	Typical Range
bool	Boolean value. It can only take one of two values: true or false.	1 byte	true or false

C Keywords			
asm	else	new	this
auto	enum	operator	throw
bool	explicit	private	TRUE
break	export	protected	try
case	extern	public	typedef
catch	FALSE	register	typeid
char	float	reinterpret_cast	typename
class	for	return	union
const	friend	short	unsigned
const_cast	goto	signed	using
continue	if	sizeof	virtual
default	inline	static	void

delete	int	static_cast	volatile
do	long	struct	wchar_t
double	mutable	switch	while
dynamic_cast	namespace	template	
In addition, the following words are also reserved:			
And	bitor	not_eq	xor
and_eq	compl	or	xor_eq
bitand	not	or_eq	

Functions	Descriptions
abort	stops the program
abs	absolute value
acos	arc cosine
asctime	a textual version of the time
asin	arc sine
assert	stops the program if an expression isn't true
atan	arc tangent
atan2	arc tangent, using signs to determine quadrants
atexit	sets a function to be called when the program exits
atof	converts a string to a double
atoi	converts a string to an integer
atol	converts a string to a long
bsearch	perform a binary search
calloc	allocates and clears a two-dimensional chunk of memory
ceil	the smallest integer not less than a certain value
clearerr	clears errors
clock	returns the amount of time that the program has been running
cos	cosine
cosh	hyperbolic cosine
ctime	returns a specifically formatted version of the time
difftime	the difference between two times
div	returns the quotient and remainder of a division
exit	stop the program

exp	returns "e" raised to a given power
fabs	absolute value for floating-point numbers
fclose	close a file
feof	true if at the end-of-file
ferror	checks for a file error
fflush	writes the contents of the output buffer
fgetc	get a character from a stream
fgetpos	get the file position indicator
fgets	get a string of characters from a stream
floor	returns the largest integer not greater than a given value
fmod	returns the remainder of a division
fopen	open a file
fprintf	print formatted output to a file
fputc	write a character to a file
fputs	write a string to a file
fread	read from a file
free	returns previously allocated memory to the operating system
freopen	open an existing stream with a different name
frexp	decomposes a number into scientific notation
fscanf	read formatted input from a file
fseek	move to a specific location in a file
fsetpos	move to a specific location in a file
ftell	returns the current file position indicator
fwrite	write to a file
getc	read a character from a file
getchar	read a character from STDIN
getenv	get environment information about a variable
gets	read a string from STDIN
gmtime	returns a pointer to the current Greenwich Mean Time
isalnum	true if a character is alphanumeric
isalpha	true if a character is alphabetic
iscntrl	true if a character is a control character
isdigit	true if a character is a digit
isgraph	true if a character is a graphical character

islower	true if a character is lowercase
isprint	true if a character is a printing character
ispunct	true if a character is punctuation
isspace	true if a character is a space character
isupper	true if a character is an uppercase character
itoa	Convert a integer to a string
isxdigit	true if a character is a hexadecimal character
labs	absolute value for long integers
ldexp	computes a number in scientific notation
ldiv	returns the quotient and remainder of a division, in long integer form
localtime	returns a pointer to the current time
log	natural logarithm
log10	natural logarithm, in base 10
longjmp	start execution at a certain point in the program
malloc	allocates memory
memchr	searches an array for the first occurrence of a character
memcmp	compares two buffers
memcpy	copies one buffer to another
memmove	moves one buffer to another
memset	fills a buffer with a character
mktime	returns the calendar version of a given time
modf	decomposes a number into integer and fractional parts
perror	displays a string version of the current error to STDERR
pow	returns a given number raised to another number
printf	write formatted output to STDOUT
putc	write a character to a stream
putchar	write a character to STDOUT
puts	write a string to STDOUT
qsort	perform a quicksort
raise	send a signal to the program
rand	returns a pseudo-random number
realloc	changes the size of previously allocated memory
remove	erase a file

rename	rename a file
rewind	move the file position indicator to the beginning of a file
scanf	read formatted input from STDIN
setbuf	set the buffer for a specific stream
setjmp	set execution to start at a certain point
setlocale	sets the current locale
setvbuf	set the buffer and size for a specific stream
signal	register a function as a signal handler
sin	sine
sinh	hyperbolic sine
sprintf	write formatted output to a buffer
sqrt	square root
srand	initialize the random number generator
sscanf	read formatted input from a buffer
strcat	concatenates two strings
strchr	finds the first occurrence of a character in a string
strcmp	compares two strings
strcoll	compares two strings in accordance to the current locale
strcpy	copies one string to another
strcspn	searches one string for any characters in another
strerror	returns a text version of a given error code
strftime	returns individual elements of the date and time
strlen	returns the length of a given string
strncat	concatenates a certain amount of characters of two strings
strncmp	compares a certain amount of characters of two strings
strncpy	copies a certain amount of characters from one string to another
strpbrk	finds the first location of any character in one string, in another string
strrchr	finds the last occurrence of a character in a string
strspn	returns the length of a substring of characters of a string
strstr	finds the first occurrence of a substring of characters

strtod	converts a string to a double
strtok	finds the next token in a string
strtol	converts a string to a long
strtoul	converts a string to an unsigned long
strxfrm	converts a substring so that it can be used by string comparison functions
system	perform a system call
tan	tangent
tanh	hyperbolic tangent
time	returns the current calendar time of the system
tmpfile	return a pointer to a temporary file
tmpnam	return a unique filename
tolower	converts a character to lowercase
toupper	converts a character to uppercase
ungetc	puts a character back into a stream
va_arg	use variable length parameter lists
vprintf, vfprintf, and vsprintf	write formatted output with variable argument lists
vscanf, vfscanf, and vsscanf	read formatted input with variable argument lists

Appendix: II

Question Bank

I.   Short Answers :

Question 1a). What is an algorithm?

Answer: A mathematician named Mohammed Ibn Musa-al-Khwarizmi first used the term: "algorithm". An **algorithm** is a list of rules to follow in order to solve a problem.

An algorithm is defined as a step-by-step procedure or method for solving a problem. Let us consider the problem of preparing a bajji. To prepare a bajji, we follow the given below steps given:

1) Get the frying pan.
2) Get the oil.
a. Do we have oil?
i. If yes, put it in the pan.
ii. If no, do we want to buy oil?
1. If yes, then go out and buy.
2. If no, we can terminate.
3) Turn on the stove, etc...

What we are doing is, for a given problem (preparing a bajji), we are providing a step-by-step procedure for solving it.

While defining an algorithm steps are written in human understandable language and independent of any programming language. We can implement it in any programming language of our choice.

Question 1b). List various input and output devices.

Answer:

Input Devices:

a)   Graphics Tablets
b)   Cameras
c)   Video Capture Hardware
d)   Trackballs
e)   Barcode reader
f)   Digital camera
g)   Gamepad
h)   Joystick
i)   Keyboard

j)　　Microphone

k)　　MIDI keyboard

l)　　Mouse (pointing device)

m)　Scanner

n)　　Webcam

o)　　Touchpads

p)　　Pen Input

q)　　Microphone

r)　　Electronic Whiteboard

s) OMR

t) OCR

u) Punch card reader

v)MICR (Magnetic Ink character reader)

w) Magnetic Tape Drive

OUTPUT DEVICES:

Monitor (LED, LCD, CRT etc)

Printers (all types)

Plotters

Projector

LCD Projection Panels

Computer Output Microfilm (COM)

Speaker(s)

Head Phone

Visual Display Unit

Film Recorder

Microfiche

Both Input–Output Devices:

Modems

Network cards

Touch Screen

　　4. Headsets (Headset consists of Speakers and Microphone.
　　　Speaker act Output Device and　　Microphone act as Input
　　　device)

　　5. Facsimile (FAX) (It has scanner to scan the document and also
　　　have printer to Print the document)

　　6.Audio Cards / Sound Card

Question 1c).   What is the significance of operating system?

Answer:

The operating system controls computer system resources and coordinates the flow of data to end from the microprocessor. At the same time, it also controls the flow of data between input and output devices such as keyboard & monitor.

Today most of the operating system perform the following function:

Processor management, Memory management, Input Output management,

File management.

Operating system is responsible for automatic transition from job to job as directed by special control statement.

It is responsible for coordination and assignment of compilers, assembler, utility programs and other software to the various users of the computer system.

It provides facility for easy communication between the computer system & the computer operator (user). It also establishes data security & integrity.

Following are the name of some operating system: -

DOS, windows, UNIX, LINUX

Question 1d).   Why switch statement is used?

Answer:

Switch statements are used when we clearly know what are possible values for the condition variable.

Each value in that list of possible value is called **case.**

When the value given in input matches the value in the case statement, the block of code below case gets executed until it reaches the **break** statement.

Break is optional. If break statement is not given, the next case statement (if any) will also get executed.

Example:
```
switch (age)
 {
  case 1:  printf("You're one.");
       break;
  case 2:  printf("You're two.");
      break;
  case 3:  printf("You're three.");
```

```
  case 4:  printf("You're three or four.");
break;
  default:
printf("You're not 1,2,3 or 4!");

}
```

Question 1e). Write down the syntax of function declaration also give an example.

Answer:

Function Declaration in C

A function (method) is a block of code that can be called from another location in the program or class. It is used to reduce the repetition of multiple lines of code.

Syntax
returnType **functionName**(parameterTypes); //*function prototype*

//*main code*

returnType **functionName** (functionParameters) { //*function implementation*
    //*statements that execute when called*
    return value;
}

Example
int findMaximum(int, int); //*prototype*

void main(){
    int maxNumber = findMaximum(5, 7); //*calling a function*
}

int findMaximum(int number1, **int** number2) { //*implementation*
    int maximum = number2;
    if (number1 > number2) maximum = number1;
    return maximum;
}

Question 1f). Draw block diagram of a computer system.

Answer:

Block diagram of computer

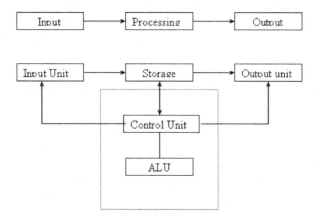

Question 1g). Differentiate syntax and logical errors.

Answer:

A syntax error is one that breaks the rules of the language. A logical error is one that may compile or run, but produces an unexpected result.

Examples:

Syntax error- not having a semicolon at the end of a statement

Example:

int a

Float b

Logical error-

A+B/2;   vs.   (A+B)/2; both give different output .

Or

Sum=A-B;

Question 1h).   Compute the binary equivalent of 357.

Answer: **101100101**

	Number/2	Result	Remainder
9	357/2	178	1
8	178/2	89	0
7	89/2	44	1
6	44/2	22	0
5	22/2	11	0
4	11/2	5	1

3	5/2	2	1
2	2/2	1	0
1	1/2	0	1

Reading from bottom: $(357)_{10} = (101100101)_2$

Question 1i) List jumping statements.

Answer:

Jumping statements are used to transfer the program's control from one location to another, these are set of keywords which are responsible to transfer program's control within the same block or from one function to another.

There are four jumping statements in C language:

- goto statement
- return statement
- break statement
- continue statement

Question 1j). Write down the syntax of else-if ladder.

Answer:
```
//Syntax of if else ladder statement
if(condition_expression_One)
 {
    statement1;
 }
 else if (condition_expression_Two)
 {
    statement2;
 }
else if (condition_expression_Three)
 {
    statement3;
 } else
 {
    statement4;
 }
```

Question 1k). Differentiate RAM and ROM.

Answer:

The difference between RAM and RAM is as follows

- RAM(random access memory) is meant for temporary storage where as ROM(read only memory) is meant for permanent storage.

- RAM chip is volatile,means once the power is turned off , it losses the previously holding information ,where as ROM is non-volatile it doesn't losses any information even though power is turned off.

- RAM chip is used in the normal operations of computer,where as ROM chip is used mainly for startup process of computer.

- Writing the data to a RAM is more faster than ROM

RAM Vs ROM

SECTION-B

2.   List and explain string library functions in detail.

Answer: A string in the C language is simply an array of characters. Strings must have a NULL or \0 character after the last character to show where the string ends. A string can be declared as a character array or with a string pointer. First we take a look at a character array example:

char mystr[20];

String I/O in C programming

```
String I/O
1) printf and scanf
2) puts and gets
Syntax of above functions - Assume string as str1

printf("%s", str1);
puts(str1);  --%s not require here.
scanf("%s", &str1);
gets(str1); --%s not require
```

C String Functions :

strlen - **Finds out the length of a string**
strlwr - **It converts a string to lowercase**
strupr - **It converts a string to uppercase**
strcat - **It appends one string at the end of another**
strncat - **It appends first n characters of a string at the end of another.**
strcpy - **Use it for Copying a string into another**
strncpy - **It copies first n characters of one string into another**
strcmp - **It compares two strings**
strncmp - **It compares first n characters of two strings**
strcmpi - **It compares two strings without regard to case ("i" denotes that this function ignores case)**
stricmp - **It compares two strings without regard to case (identical to strcmpi)**
strnicmp - **It compares first n characters of two strings, Its not case sensitive**
strdup - **Used for Duplicating a string**
strchr - **Finds out first occurrence of a given character in a string**
strrchr - **Finds out last occurrence of a given character in a string**
strstr - **Finds first occurrence of a given string in another string**
strset - **It sets all characters of string to a given character**
strnset - **It sets first n characters of a string to a given character**
strrev - **It Reverses a string**

Question 3. Write the following programs

a.   To determine whether a number is palindrome.

b.   To compute transpose of a matrix.

Answer: a) // To determine whether a number is palindrome.

```
1.    #include <stdio.h>
2.
3.    int main()
4.    {
5.      int n, reverse = 0, t;
6.
7.      printf("Enter a number to check if it is a palindrome or not\n");
8.      scanf("%d", &n);
9.
10.     t = n;
```

```
11.
12.      while (t != 0)
13.      {
14.        reverse = reverse * 10;
15.        reverse = reverse + t%10;
16.        t = t/10;
17.      }
18.
19.      if (n == reverse)
20.        printf("%d is a palindrome number.\n", n);
21.      else
22.        printf("%d isn't a palindrome number.\n", n);
23.
24.      return 0;
25.    }
```

Answer b) // To compute transpose of a matrix.

Transpose of a matrix in C

Transpose of a matrix in C language: This C program prints transpose of a matrix. It is obtained by interchanging rows and columns of a matrix. For example, consider the following 3 X 2 matrix:

1 2
3 4
5 6

Transpose of the matrix:

1 3 5
2 4 6

When we transpose a matrix then its order changes, but for a square matrix it remains the same.

C program to find transpose of a matrix

```
1.      #include <stdio.h>
2.
3.      int main()
4.      {
5.        int m, n, c, d, matrix[10][10], transpose[10][10];
6.
7.        printf("Enter the number of rows and columns of matrix\n");
8.        scanf("%d%d", &m, &n);
```

```
9.
10.     printf("Enter elements of the matrix\n");
11.
12.     for (c = 0; c < m; c++)
13.       for(d = 0; d < n; d++)
14.         scanf("%d", &matrix[c][d]);
15.
16.     for (c = 0; c < m; c++)
17.       for( d = 0 ; d < n ; d++ )
18.         transpose[d][c] = matrix[c][d];
19.
20.     printf("Transpose of the matrix:\n");
21.
22.     for (c = 0; c < n; c++) {
23.       for (d = 0; d < m; d++)
24.         printf("%d\t", transpose[c][d]);
25.       printf("\n");
26.     }
27.
28.     return 0;
29.   }
```

Output of program:

Question 4. Differentiate call by value and call by reference with programming example.

Answer:

Difference between Call by Value and Call by Reference in C

S. No.	Call by Value	Call by Reference
1.	A copy of actual parameters is passed into formal parameters.	Reference of actual parameters is passed into formal parameters.
2.	Changes in formal parameters will not result in changes in actual parameters.	Changes in formal parameters will result in changes in actual parameters.
3.	Separate memory location is allocated for actual and formal parameters.	Same memory location is allocated for actual and formal parameters.

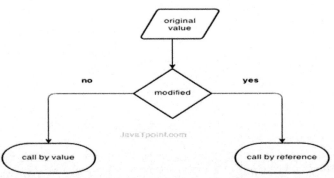

```
#include<stdio.h>
void fun(int x)
{
    x=x+5;
}
int main()
{
    int a=10;
    printf("Before calling\na=%d",a);
    fun(a);
    printf("\n\nAfter calling\na=%d",a);
    return 0;
}
```

Output:

```
C:\Users\TCP\Documents\demo.exe

Before calling
a=10

After calling
a=10
------------------------------------------------
Process exited with return value 0
Press any key to continue . . .
```

```c
#include<stdio.h>

void fun(int *x)
{
    *x=(*x)+5;
}

int main()
{
    int a=10;
    printf("Before calling\na=%d",a);
    fun(&a);
    printf("\n\nAfter calling\na=%d",a);

    return 0;
}
```

Output:

```
C:\Users\TCP\Documents\demo.exe

Before calling
a=10

After calling
a=15
------------------------------------------------
Process exited with return value 0
Press any key to continue . . . _
```

Question 5. Write a program to search an element from a list of numbers.
Answer:
//Linear search or sequential search C program

```c
#include <stdio.h>
int main()
{
  int array[100], search, c, n;
  printf("Enter number of elements in array\n");
  scanf("%d", &n);
  printf("Enter %d integer(s)\n", n);
  for (c = 0; c < n; c++)
    scanf("%d", &array[c]);
  printf("Enter a number to search\n");
  scanf("%d", &search);
  for (c = 0; c < n; c++)
  {
    if (array[c] == search)    /* If required element is found */
    {
      printf("%d is present at location %d.\n", search, c+1);
      break;
    }
  }
  if (c == n)
    printf("%d isn't present in the array.\n", search);
  return 0;
}
```

Output of program:

```
E:\programmingsimplified.com\c\linear-search.exe

Enter the number of elements in array
5
Enter 5 numbers
5
6
4
2
9
Enter the number to search
4
4 is present at location 3.
```

SECTION-C

6.   What do you mean by recursion? Give programming illustration to represent the concept

of recursion.

Answer:

"Recursion is a process in which a problem is define in terms of itself".

The problem is solved by repetitively breaking it into smaller problem which are similar in nature to the original problem.

Advantages of Recursion:

1. Reduce unnecessary calling of function.

2. Through Recursion one can Solve problems in easy way while its iterative solution is very big and complex.For example to reduce the code size for Tower of Honai application, a recursive function is bet suited.

3. Extremely useful when applying the same solution.

Disadvantages of Recursion:

1. Recursive solution is always logical and it is very difficult to trace.(debug and understand).

2. In recursive we must have an if statement somewhere to force the function to return without the recursive call being executed, otherwise the function will never return.

3. Recursion takes a lot of stack space, usually not considerable when the program is small and running on a PC.

4. Recursion uses more processor time.

Example of Factorial Program using Recursion:

```
#include<stdio.h>
int find_factorial(int);
int main()
{
  int num, fact;
  //Ask user for the input and store it in num
  printf("\nEnter any integer number:");
  scanf("%d",&num);

  //Calling our user defined function
```

```
  fact =find_factorial(num);

  //Displaying factorial of input number
  printf("\nfactorial of %d is: %d" ,num, fact);
  return 0;
}
int find_factorial(int n)
{
  //Factorial of 0 is 1
  if(n==0)
    return(1);

  //Function calling itself: recursion
  return(n*find_factorial(n-1));
}
```

7.   **Write a program to sort a list of numbers using bubble sort method.**

8.   **Explain the following operators with example**

a.   **Relational**

b.   **Conditional**

c.   **Logical**

d.   **Arithmetic**

Answer:

Operators in C language are symbols which tells the compiler to perform some mathematical calculations or logical operations on the variables and constants.

a)   Relational operator

Relational operators are binary operators(operates on two operands) and are used to relate or compare two operands. There are four relational operators in C (i.e <, <=, >, >=). If the relationship between the operands is correct, it will return 1 and returns 0 otherwise.

Apart from four relational operators, C has two equality operator (== and !=) as well for comparing operands. Now let's take a look at different relational and equality operators and how they operate on the operands.

Operator	Name	Description	Example
<	'Less than' operator	Checks if the first operand is less than second operand and returns 1 if it's true, else returns 0	10 < 5 returns 0 and 5 < 10 returns 1
<=	'Less than or equals to' operator	Checks if the first operand is less than or equals to second operand and returns 1 if it's true, else returns 0	10 <= 10 returns 1 and 10 <= 5 returns 0
>	'Greater than' operator	Checks if the first operand is greater than second operand and returns 1 if it's true, else returns 0	10 > 5 returns 1 and 5 > 10 returns 0
>=	'Greater than or equals to' operator	Checks if the first operand is greater than or equals to second operand and returns 1 if it's true, else returns 0	10 >= 10 returns 1 and 5 >= 10 returns 0
==	Equality operator	Checks if the two operands are equal are returns 1 if it's true, else returns 0	10 == 10 returns 1 and 10 == 1 returns 0
!=	Non-equality operator	Checks if the two operands are equal are returns 1 if they are not equal, else returns 0	10 != 10 returns 0 and 10 != 1 returns 1

b) Conditional Operator :   C Ternary Operator (?:)

A conditional operator is a ternary operator, that is, it works on 3 operands.

Conditional Operator Syntax

conditionalExpression ? expression1 : expression2

The conditional operator works as follows:

*   The first expression conditionalExpression is evaluated first. This expression evaluates to 1 if it's true and evaluates to 0 if it's false.

*   If *conditionalExpression* is true, *expression1* is evaluated.

*   If *conditionalExpression* is false, *expression2* is evaluated.

Example #7: C conditional Operator

```
#include <stdio.h>
int main(){
  char February;
  int days;
  printf("If this year is leap year, enter 1. If not enter any integer: ");
  scanf("%c",&February);
```

```
// If test condition (February == '1') is true, days equal to 29.
// If test condition (February =='1') is false, days equal to 28.
days = (February == '1') ? 29 : 28;
printf("Number of days in February = %d",days);
return 0;
}
```

Output

If this year is leap year, enter 1. If not enter any integer: 1

Number of days in February = 29

c) Logical operator

We've learned about relational operators, using which we can do comparisons. What if you need to combine two relational expressions, for example, *if you want to check if a number is greater than 10 and less than 20?* You can use logical operators for that purpose. There are three logical operators in C language, &&, ||, !. Details and examples of logical operators are given below

Operator	Name	Description	Example
&&	'Logical AND' Operator	'AND' operator returns true if both the operands it operates on evaluates to true (non-zero), else return false	a && b returns true if both a and b are non-zero
||	'Logical OR' Operator	'OR' operator returns true if any of the operands it operates on evaluates to true (non-zero), else return false	a || b returns true if either a or b are non-zero
!	'Logical NOT' Operator	'NOT' operator is a unary operator (it operates only on one operand). It returns true if the operand is false and returns false if the operand is true	!a returns true if a is false. Else returns false

d) Arithmetic Operators

Arithmetic operators are used to perform basic mathematical operations like addition, subtraction, multiplication and division. There are five arithmetic operators available in C (+, -, *, /, %). All arithmetic operators are binary operators, ie; they operate on two operands to produce the result.

The table below lists the arithmetic operators

Operator	Name	Description	Example
+	Addition Operator	'+' Operator adds two values. This operator works on integer, float and character variables.	20 + 10return 20
-	Subtraction Operator	'-' Operator produces a result after subtracting two values. It also works on integer, float, character variables.	20 - 10returns 10
*	Multiplication Operator	'*' Operator produces result after multiplication of operands.	20 * 10returns 200
/	Division Operator	'/' Operator produces result of division of first operand by second.	20 / 10returns 2
&	Modulus Operator	'%' Operator generates the remainder after integer division.	25 % 10returns 5

9. Explain the concept of array of structure with programming illustration.

Answer:

Array of Structures

A structure is a composite datatype with a collection of variables. These variables can have different data types and collectively form a structure of a composite datatype. An array of structures is a sequential collection of structures. With structures, you can store mixed record types and with an array supporting this, you can have a list of mixed record types. The following example shows a structure called *student* that takes the roll number and name of a student as an input. It then stores each record in an array *st*, which stores three elements. Each element will hold a mixed record.

```
1.  #include<stdio.h>
2.  #include <string.h>
3.  struct student{
4.    int rollno;
5.    char name[10];
6.  };
7.  int main(){
8.    int i;
9.    struct student st[3];
10.   printf("Enter Records of 3 students");
```

```
11.   for(i=0;i<3;i++){
12.   printf("\nEnter Rollno:");    scanf("%d",&st[i].rollno);    printf("\nEnter
Name:");  scanf("%s",&st[i].name);
13.   }
14.   printf("\nStudent Information List:");
15.   for(i=0;i<3;i++){   printf("\nRollno:%d, Name:%s",st[i].rollno,st[i].name);
16.   }
17.   return 0;
18.   }
```

University Question Papers

Section-A

Q1. Write notes on:

a) What is the syntax of If statement?

Answer:

b) What is the syntax of Switch statement?

c) What the syntax is of do while statement?

d) What is a Pointer?

e) What is the scope of Local Variable?

f) What are the conditional Operators available in C?

g) What is RAM?

h) What is a Compiler?

i) What are the syntax of PRINTF statements of C?

j) What is the need for Operating system?

Section-B

Q2. What is an Operating System? What do you mean by booting? Also explain what is meant by loading, saving, compiling & execution of a program?

Q3. Explain the Block diagram of a Computer. Also explain the difference between primary memory and secondary memory.

Q4. What is a flow chart? Draw flow chart to find the smallest of three numbers.

Q5. What are the various applications of computers?

Section-C

Q6. Write a program to reverse the digits of a number and sum of Digits.

Q7. What are the user defined data types in C ? Explain with example.

Q8. Write a program using functions to find the all types of a quadratics equation.

Q9. Write a program to find the sum of two Matrices.

Appendix : III

Practice C++ Lab Programs

Appendix : III

Practice C++ Lab Programs

Practical No	Practical Name
5	WAP to display message on screen.
6	WAP to perform addition of two numbers.
7	WAP to perform all arithmetical operations (+,-,*,/, %).
8	WAP to calculate area of circle and area of rectangle.
9	WAP to swap two numbers.
10	WAP to calculate total marks of student and percentage.
11	WAP to convert temperature in Fahrenheit to Centigrade.
12	WAP to find out whether the given number is even or odd
13	WAP to convert a given numbers of days into years, weeks and days.
14	WAP to find out greater out of two numbers
15	WAP to input a character and to print whether a given character is an upper case or lower case, digit or any other character.
16	WAP to find out greatest out of three numbers using nested if.
17	WAP to calculate roots of a quadratic equation $ax^2 +bx+c=0 (a!=0)$
18	WAP to perform arithmetical operators using switch statement.
19	WAP to print ten natural number and their sum by using:- (a) For loop (b) While loop (c) Do while loop
20	WAP to print table of a number using any loop.
21	WAP to find out factorial of a number.
22	WAP to generate Fibonacci series.
23	WAP to check whether the given no is prime or not.
24	WAP to find out reverse of a given number.
25	WAP to check out whether the given no is palindrome or not.
26	WAP a program to print following pattern : * ** *** ****
27	WAP to find addition of two numbers using functions.
28	WAP to find out cube of a given no. using function.
29	WAP to find out swapping of two numbers using call by value.
30	WAP to find out swapping of two numbers using call by reference.
31	WAP to read and write an 1-D array.
32	WAP to read and write an 2-D array.
33	WAP to multiply two matrix.
34	WAP to perform various String manipulation functions (strcat, strlen,strrev,strcmp).
35	WAP to find out factorial of a number using recursion.
36	Create a class named student with the appropriate data members and member functions to generate output comprising student's admission

no.,name,marks in five subjects and the %age of marks obtained. WAP to use the student class.

Experiment 5

WAP to display message on screen.

5. //Generate a program to print Hello C++.

```
#include<iostream.h>
#include<conio.h>
void main()
{
 clrscr();
cout<<"Hello C++ ";
getch();
}
```

....

OUTPUT:

....

Hello C++

Experiment 6

WAP to perform addition of two numbers

```
#include<iostream.h>
#include<conio.h>
void main()
{
 clrscr();
long int a , b, add ;
cout<<"Enter the numbers a and b : ";
cin>>a>>b;
add=a+b;

cout<<"Addition = " << add   ;
getch();
}
```
....
OUTPUT:
....
Enter the numbers a and b :
5
7
Addition = 12

Experiment 7

WAP to perform all arithmetical operations (+,-,*,/, %)

```
#include<iostream.h>
#include<conio.h>
void main()
{
clrscr();
float a,b,res;
int ch,q;
cout<<"Arithmetic Operatios";
cout<<"nn1.Additionn2.Subtractionn3.Multiplicationn4.Divisionn5.Mode";
cout<<"n Enter your choice:";
cin>>ch;

switch(ch)
```

```cpp
{
case 1:
{
cout<<"nnEnter two variables:";
cin>>a>>b;
res=a+b;
cout<<"n  Result="<<res;
}
break;

case 2:
{
cout<<"nnEnter two variables:";
cin>>a>>b;
res=a-b;
cout<<"n  Result="<<res;
}
break;
case 3:
{
cout<<"nnEnter two variables:";
cin>>a>>b;
res=a*b;
cout<<"n  Result="<<res;
}
break;

case 4:
{
cout<<"nnEnter two variables:";
cin>>a>>b;
if(a>=b)
{
res=a/b;
cout<<"n  Result="<<res;
}
else
cout<<"nnt1st varable should be greater than 2nd.!!!";
}
```

```
break;

case 5:
{
cout<<"nnEnter two variables:";
cin>>a>>b;
if(a>=b)
{
q=a/b;
res=a-(b*q);
cout<<"n  Result="<<res;
}
else
cout<<"nnt1st variable should be greater than 2nd..!!!";
}
break;
}

getch();
}
```

Experiment 8

8a. //Generate a program to find area of a circle.

```
#include<iostream.h>
#include<conio.h>
void main()
{
clrscr();
float a,r;
cout<<"Enter the value of radius: ";
cin>>r;
a=3.14*r*r;
cout<<"The area of circle is: "<<a;
getch();
}
```
....
OUTPUT:
....

Enter the value of radius: 5

The area of circle is: 78.5

8b. //Generate a program to find area of Rectangle.

```
#include<iostream.h>
#include<conio.h>
void main()
{
clrscr();
float l,b,area
cout<<"Enter the length and width of rectangle : ";
cin>>l>>b;
area=l*b;
cout<<"The area of Rectangle is: "<<area;
getch();
}
```
....

OUTPUT:

....

Enter the length and width of rectangle:

4

5

The area of Rectangle is:

20

Experiment 9

WAP to swap two numbers

```
#include<iostream.h>
#include<conio.h>
void main()
{
 clrscr();
int a,b,temp;
```

```
cout<<"Enter a: ";
cin>>a;
cout<<"Enter b: ";
cin>>b;
temp=a;
a=b;
b=temp;
cout<<"The numbers are swapped"<<'\n'<<"Now a="<<a<<'\n'<<"And b="<<b;
getch();
}
```
....

OUTPUT:

....

Enter a: 56
Enter b: 78
The numbers are swapped
Now a=78
And b=56

Experiment 10

WAP to calculate total marks of student and percentage.

```
#include<stdio.h>
#include<conio.h>
int main()
{
clrscr();
int s1,s2,s3,s4,s5,total,per;
printf("Enter the marks of 5 subjects:\nEach contain 100 marks:\n");
scanf("%d%d%d%d%d",&s1,&s2,&s3,&s4,&s5);
total=s1+s2+s3+s4+s5;
per=total/5;
printf("total marks in 5 subject=%d\n",total);
printf("percentage marks obtained in 5 subjects=%d",per);
getch();
return 0;

}
```

Experiment 11

WAP to convert temperature in Fahrenheit to Centigrade

```
#include<conio.h>
#include<iostream.h>
void main()
{
float f,c;
clrscr();
cout<<"Enter Fahrenheit degree to find temperature in celsius: ";
cin>>f;
c = (f-32)/1.8;   // FORMULA    C = F-32 / 1.8

cout<<"\n\n\tCELSIUS DEGREE = "<<c;
getch();
```

Experiment 12

WAP to find out whether the given number is even or odd

```
#include<iostream.h>
#include<conio.h>
void main()
{
clrscr();
int a;
cout<<"Enter the value of the number: ";
cin>>a;
if((a%2)!=0)
    {
cout<<"The number entered is odd";
}
else
    {
cout<<"The number entered is even";
}
getch();
}
```

....
OUTPUT:
....

Enter the value of the number: 57
The number entered is odd

Experiment 13

WAP to convert a given numbers of days into years, weeks and days

```cpp
#include<iostream.h>
#include<conio.h>
int main()
{
clrscr();
int totdays,years,weeks,days,num;
cout<<"\n\t Enter the total number of days:";
cin>>totdays;
years=totdays/365;
num=totdays%365;
weeks=num/7;
days=num%7;
cout<<"\n";
cout<<"Years="<<years<<","<<"Weeks="<<weeks<<","<<"Days="<<days<<"\
n";
return 0;
}
```

Experiment 14

WAP to find out greater out of two numbers

```cpp
//Write a program to find greater between two numbers
#include <iostream.h>
#include <conio.h>
void main ()
{
int a,b;
clrscr ();
cout <<"Enter A: ";
```

```
cin >>a;
cout <<"Enter B: ";
cin >>b;
if (a>b)
{
cout <<"A is Greater";
}
else
{
cout <<"B is Greater";
}
getch ();
}
```

Experiment 15

WAP to input a character and to print whether a given character is an upper case or lower case, digit or any other character.

```
#include<iostream.h>
#include<conio.h>
void main()
{      clrscr();
char ch;
cout<<"Enter any character";
cin>>ch;
if(ch>=65&&ch<=90)
cout<<endl<<"You enterd a uppercase character";
else
if(ch>=48&&ch<=57)
cout<<endl<<"You enterd a digit";
else
if(ch>=97&&ch<=122)
cout<<endl<<"You enterd a lowercase character";
else
cout<<endl<<"You enterd a special character";
getch();
}
```

Experiment 16

WAP to find out greatest out of three numbers using nested if

```cpp
#include <iostream>
using namespace std;

int main() {

    float n1, n2, n3;
    cout << "Enter three numbers: ";
    cin >> n1 >> n2 >> n3;
    if(n1>=n2 && n1>=n3) {
        cout << "Largest number: " << n1;
    }
    if(n2>=n1 && n2>=n3) {
        cout << "Largest number: " << n2;
    }
    if(n3>=n1 && n3>=n2) {
        cout << "Largest number: " << n3;
    }

    return 0;
}
```

Experiment 17

WAP to calculate roots of a quadratic equation $ax^2 + bx + c = 0 (a != 0)$

```cpp
#include <iostream>
#include <cmath>
using namespace std;

int main() {

    float a, b, c, x1, x2, determinant, realPart, imaginaryPart;
    cout << "Enter coefficients a, b and c: ";
    cin >> a >> b >> c;
    determinant = b*b - 4*a*c;
```

```cpp
    if (determinant > 0) {
        x1 = (-b + sqrt(determinant)) / (2*a);
        x2 = (-b - sqrt(determinant)) / (2*a);
        cout << "Roots are real and different." << endl;
        cout << "x1 = " << x1 << endl;
        cout << "x2 = " << x2 << endl;
    }

    else if (determinant == 0) {
        cout << "Roots are real and same." << endl;
        x1 = (-b + sqrt(determinant)) / (2*a);
        cout << "x1 = x2 =" << x1 << endl;
    }

    else {
        realPart = -b/(2*a);
        imaginaryPart =sqrt(-determinant)/(2*a);
        cout << "Roots are complex and different."  << endl;
        cout << "x1 = " << realPart << "+" << imaginaryPart << "i" << endl;
        cout << "x2 = " << realPart << "-" << imaginaryPart << "i" << endl;
    }

    return 0;
}
```

Output

Enter coefficients a, b and c: 4

5

1

Roots are real and different.

x1 = -0.25

x2 = -1

Experiment 18

WAP to perform arithmetical operators using switch statement

```cpp
#include<iostream.h>
#include<conio.h>
void main()
{
clrscr();
float a,b,res;
int ch,q;
cout<<"Arithmetic Operatios";
cout<<"nn1.Additionn2.Subtractionn3.Multiplicationn4.Divisionn5.Mode";
cout<<"n  Enter your choice:";
cin>>ch;

switch(ch)
{
case 1:
{
cout<<"nnEnter two variables:";
cin>>a>>b;
res=a+b;
cout<<"n  Result="<<res;
}
break;

case 2:
{
cout<<"nnEnter two variables:";
cin>>a>>b;
res=a-b;
cout<<"n  Result="<<res;
}
break;

case 3:
{
cout<<"nnEnter two variables:";
cin>>a>>b;
```

```
res=a*b;
cout<<"n  Result="<<res;
}
break;

case 4:
{
cout<<"nnEnter two variables:";
cin>>a>>b;
if(a>=b)
{
res=a/b;
cout<<"n  Result="<<res;
}
else
cout<<"nnt1st varable should be greater than 2nd.!!!";
}
break;

case 5:
{
cout<<"nnEnter two variables:";
cin>>a>>b;
if(a>=b)
{
q=a/b;
res=a-(b*q);
cout<<"n  Result="<<res;
}
else
cout<<"nnt1st variable should be greater than 2nd..!!!";
}
break;
}

getch();

}
```

Experiment 19

WAP to print ten natural number and their sum by using:-

(a)   **For loop**
(b)   **While loop**
(c)   **Do while loop**
19a.)   // By using For loop

```cpp
#include <iostream>
using namespace std;

int main() {

    int n, sum = 0;
    cout << "Enter a positive integer: ";
    cin >> n;
    for (int i = 1; i <= n; ++i) {
        sum += i;
    }
    cout << "Sum = " << sum;
    return 0;
}
```

19 b) // By Using While loop

```cpp
#include <iostream>

int currentSum;
int counter;

int main() {

currentSum = 0;
counter = 1;

while (counter < 11)

{
currentSum = currentSum + counter;
counter = counter + 1;
```

```
}

printf("The sum is %i",currentSum);

}
```

19c) // By Using do while loop

```
#include<stdio.h>
#include<conio.h>
void main()
{
int i,n,sum=0;
clrscr();
printf("enter the how many terms\n");
scanf("%d",&n);

i=1;
do
{
  printf("%4d",i);
   sum=sum+i;
  i++;
}
while(i<=n);
printf("\n\nsum=%d\n",sum);
getch();
}
```

Experiment 20

WAP to print table of a number using any loop

```
#include<iostream.h>
#include<conio.h>
void main()
{ clrscr();
int a,i;
cout<<"Enter a number to generate its table: ";
cin>>a;
for(i=1;i<=10;i++)
cout<<'\n'<<a<<"x"<<i<<"="<<a*i;
```

```
getch();
}
```
....

OUTPUT:

Enter a number to generate its table: 3

3x1=3

3x2=6

3x3=9

3x4=12

3x5=15

3x6=18

3x7=21

3x8=24

3x9=27

3x10=30

Experiment 21

WAP to find out factorial of a number

```
#include<iostream.h>
#include<conio.h>
void main()
{
 clrscr();
long int i,n;
long int fact=1;
cout<<"Enter the number whose factorial you want to find: ";
cin>>n;
for(i=2;i<=n;i++)
{
fact=fact*i;
}
cout<<"The factorial of given number is: "<<fact;
getch();
}
```
....

OUTPUT:

....

Enter the number whose factorial you want to find: 5

The factorial of given number is: 120

Experiment 22

WAP to generate Fibonacci series

```cpp
#include<iostream>

using namespace std;

main()
{
  int n, c, first = 0, second = 1, next;

  cout << "Enter the number of terms of Fibonacci series you want" << endl;
  cin >> n;

  cout << "First " << n << " terms of Fibonacci series are :- " << endl;

  for ( c = 0 ; c < n ; c++ )
  {
    if ( c <= 1 )
      next = c;
    else
    {
      next = first + second;
      first = second;
      second = next;
    }
    cout << next << endl;
  }

  return 0;
}
```

Experiment 23

WAP to check whether the given no is prime or not

```cpp
#include<iostream.h>
#include<conio.h>

int main()
{
        clrscr();
        int num;
        int i=2;
        cout<<"\n\n\tEnter a Number :::\t";
        cin>>num;

        while(i<=num-1)
        {
            if(num%i==0)
            {
                    cout<<"\n\n\t"<<num<<" is not a prime number";
                    break;
            }
            i++;
        }
        if(i==num)
        {
            cout<<"\n\n\t"<<num<<" is prime number";
        }
        getch();
}
```

Experiment 24

WAP to find out reverse of a given number

```cpp
#include<iostream.h>
#include<conio.h>

void main()
{
clrscr(); //to clear the screen
long n,rev=0,d;
```

```cpp
cout<<"Enter the number:";
cin>>n;

while(n!=0)
{
d=n%10;
rev=(rev*10)+d;
n=n/10;
}

cout<<"The reversed number is "<<rev;
getch(); //to stop the screen
}
```

Experiment 25

WAP to check out whether the given no is palindrome or not

```cpp
/* C++ program to check whether a number is palindrome or not */

#include <iostream>
using namespace std;

int main()
{
  int n, num, digit, rev = 0;
    cout << "Enter a positive number: ";
    cin >> num;
    n = num;
    do
    {
       digit = num%10;
       rev = (rev*10) + digit;
       num = num/10;
    }while (num!=0);
    cout << " The reverse of the number is: " << rev << endl;
    if (n==rev)
      cout << " The number is a palindrome";
    else
```

cout << " The number is not a palindrome";

   return 0;

}

Output

Enter a positive number: 12321
The reverse of the number is: 12321
The number is a palindrome

Experiment 26

WAP a program to print following pattern :

```
*
**
***
****
```

```cpp
#include<iostream.h>
#include<conio.h>
void main()
{
clrscr();
for(int i=1;i<=4;i++)
{
        for(int j=1;j<=i;j++)
        {
cout<<'*';
}
cout<<'\n';
}
getch();
}
```
....
OUTPUT:
....
```
*
**
***
****
```

Experiment 27

WAP to find addition of two numbers using functions

```
#include<iostream.h>
#include<conio.h>
long add(long a,long b)
{
return (a+b);
}
void main()
{
clrscr();
long add(long a,long b);
long num1, num2;
cout<<"Enter the first number: ";
cin>>num1;
cout<<"Enter the second number: ";
cin>>num2;
cout<<"The sum of the two numbers you have entered is: "<<add(num1,num2);
getch();
}
```

....
OUTPUT:
....

Enter the first number: 34
Enter the second number: 56
The sum of the two numbers you have entered is: 90

Experiment 28

WAP to find out cube of a given no. using function

```
#include<iostream.h>
#include<conio.h>
void                                              main()
{
clrscr();                                    //to clear screen
float  cube(float);                          //function prototype
float                                             a,cu;
cout<<"Enter                 any              number:";
cin>>a;
cu=cube(a);                                  //function calling
cout<<"nCube        of        "<<a<<"     is        "<<cu;
getch();
}
float                    cube(float                        a)
{
float                                             cu;
cu=a*a*a;
return(cu);
}
```

Experiment 29

WAP to find out swapping of two numbers using call by value

```
#include<iostream.h>
#include<conio.h>
void swap(int x, int y)
{
int t = x;
x = y;
y = t;
cout << "After swap in a swap function\na= " << x <<"\nb= "<<y;
}
void main()
{
    int a,b;
```

```
cout <<"Enter first no\n"   ;
cin >> a;
cout <<"Enter second no\n"   ;
cin >>b;
swap(a,b);
cout << "\n\nAfter swap without reference& in main function\na= " << a
<<"\nb= "<<b;
getch();
}
```

Experiment 30

WAP to find out swapping of two numbers using call by reference

```
#include<iostream.h>
#include<conio.h>
void swap (int &a, int &b)
{
   /* &a and &b are reference variables */
int temp;
   temp=a;
   a=b;
   b=temp;
}

main()
{
   clrscr();
   int i=5,j=10;
   cout<<"Before swapping I = "<<i<<" J = "<<j<<endl;
   swap(i,j);
   cout<<"After swapping I = "<<i<<" J = "<<j<<endl;
}
```

Experiment 31

WAP to read and write a 1-D array

```
#include<stdio.h>
#include<conio.h>
void main()
{
        clrscr();
        int arr[50], n;
        cout<<"How many element you want to store in the array ? ";
        cin>>n;
        cout<<"Enter "<<n<<" element to store in the array : ";
        for(int i=0; i<n; i++)
        {
                cin>>arr[i];
        }
        cout<<"The Elements in the Array is : \n";
        for(i=0; i<n; i++)
        {
                cout<<arr[i]<<" ";
        }
        getch();
}
```

Experiment 32

WAP to read and write a 2-D array

```
#include <iostream>
using namespace std;
void print(int A[][3],int N, int M)
{
  for (R = 0; R < N; R++)
   for (C = 0; C < M; C++)
     cout << A[R][C];
}

int main ()
{
  int arr[4][3] ={{12, 29, 11},
```

```
        {25, 25, 13},
        {24, 64, 67},
        {11, 18, 14}}};
   print(arr,4,3);
   return 0;
}
```

Experiment 33

WAP to multiply two matrix

```
#include<iostream.h>
#include<conio.h>
void main()
{
clrscr();
int a[5][5],b[5][5],c[5][5],m,n,p,q,i,j,k;
cout<<"Enter rows and columns of first matrix:";
cin>>m>>n;
cout<<"Enter rows and columns of second matrix:";
cin>>p>>q;

if(n==p)
{
cout<<"nEnter first matrix:n";
for(i=0;i<m;++i)
for(j=0;j<n;++j)
cin>>a[i][j];

cout<<"nEnter second matrix:n";
for(i=0;i<p;++i)
for(j=0;j<q;++j)
cin>>b[i][j];
cout<<"nThe new matrix is:n";

for(i=0;i<m;++i)
{
for(j=0;j<q;++j)
{
c[i][j]=0;
for(k=0;k<n;++k)
```

```
c[i][j]=c[i][j]+(a[i][k]*b[k][j]);
cout<<c[i][j]<<" ";
}
cout<<"n";
}
}
else
cout<<"nSorry!!!! Matrix multiplication can't be done";
getch();
}
```

Experiment 34

WAP to perform various String manipulation functions

(strcat, strlen,strrev,strcmp)

```
#include<iostream.h>
#include<conio.h>
#include<string.h>
void main()
{
char s1[20],s2[20],i;
clrscr();
cout<<"Enter the string to find the length:";
cin>>s1;
cout<<"\nLength of the string is..."<<strlen(s1);

strcpy(s2,s1);
cout<<"\n\nCopied string is..."<<s2;

cout<<"\n\nEnter 2 strings to be concatenated:";
cin>>s1>>s2;
strcat(s1,s2);
cout<<"\nConcatenated string is..."<<s1<<endl;

cout<<endl<<"\nEnter 2 strings to be compared:";
cin>>s1>>s2;
i=strcmp(s1,s2);
if(i==0)
```

```
cout<<"\nBoth strings are equal\n";
else if(i<0)
cout<<s1<<" is less than "<<s2<<endl;
else
 cout<<s1<<" is greater than "<<s2;

cout<<"\n\nEnter the string to change into lower case:";
cin>>s1;
cout<<"\nLower case of the given string is..."<<strlwr(s1);

cout<<"\n\nEnter the string to change into upper case:";
cin>>s1;
cout<<"\nUpper case of the given string is..."<<strupr(s1);

cout<<"\n\nEnter the string to be reversed:";
cin>>s1;
cout<<"\nThe reversed string is..."<<strrev(s1);
getch();
}
```

Experiment 35

WAP to find out factorial of a number using recursion

```
#include<iostream.h>
#include<conio.h>
void main()
{
        int n,fact;
        int rec(int); clrscr();
        cout<<"Enter the number:->";
        cin>>n;
        fact=rec(n);
        cout<<endl<<"Factorial Result are:: "<<fact<<endl;
        getch();
}
rec(int x)
{
        int f;
        if(x==1)
```

```
                return(x);
        else
        {
                f=x*rec(x-1);
                return(f);
        }
}
```

Experiment 36

Create a class named student with the appropriate data members and member functions to generate output comprising student's admission no.,name,marks in five subjects and the %age of marks obtained.

WAP to use the student class.

```
#include<iostream.h>
#include<stdio.h>
#include<dos.h>
class student
{
        int roll;
        char name[25];
        char add [25];
        char *city;
        public: student()
        {
                cout<<"welcome in the student information system"<<endl;
        }
        void getdata()
        {
                cout<<"\n enter the student roll no.";
                cin>>roll;
                cout<<"\n enter the student name";
                cin>>name;
                cout<<\n enter ther student address";
                cin>>add;
                cout<<"\n enter the student city";
                cin>>city;
        }
        void putdata()
```

```cpp
        {
                cout<,"\n the student roll no:"<<roll;
                cout<<"\n the student name:"<<name;
                cout<<"\n the student coty:"<<city;
        }
};
class mrks: public student
{
        int sub1;
        int sub2;
        int sub3;
        int per;
        public: void input()
        {
                getdata();
                cout<<"\n enter the marks1:"
                cin>>sub1:
                cout<<"\n enter the marks2:";
                cin>>sub2;
                cout<<\n enter the marks3:";
                cin>>sub3;
        }
        void output()
        {
                putdata();
                cout<<"\n marks1:"<<sub1;
                cout<<"\n marks2:"<<sub2;
                cout<<"\n marks3:"<<sub3;
        }
        void calculate ()
        {
                per= (sub1+sub2+sub3)/3;
                cout<<"\n tottal percentage"<<per;
        }
};

void main()
{
        marks m1[25];
```

```
int ch;
int count=0;
do
{
        cout<<"\n1.input data";
        cout<<"\n2.output data";
        cout<<"\n3. Calculate percentage";
        cout<<"\n4.exit";
        cout<<"\n enter the choice";
        cin>>ch;
        switch (ch)
        {
                case 1:
                m1.input();
                count++;
                break;

            case2:
                m1.output();
                break;

                case3:
                m1.calculate();
                break;
        }
    } while (ch!=4);
}
```

Experiment 37

C++ program to find HCF and LCM of two numbers

```
# include <iostream>
# include <string >
using namespace std;
int main()
{
int a,b,c;
cout<< "Enter two nos :"<<endl;
```

```
cout<<endl;
cout<< "Enter first no. : ";
cin>>a;
cout<< "Enter sec. no. : ";
cin>>b;
c=a*b;
while(a!=b)
{
if(a>b)
a=a-b;
else
b=b-a;
}
cout<< "HCF = " << a<<endl;
cout<< "LCM = " << c/a<<endl;
return 0;
}
```

Experiment 38

WAP for sort an array in Ascending or Descending order by using Bubble Sort

```
#include<iostream.h>
#include<conio.h>
void main()
{
int i,j,size,name[20],temp;
cout<<"\nHow many numbers:";
cin>>size;

cout<<"\nEnter the 1 d arrays:";
for(i=0;i<size;i++)
{
cin>>name[i];
}
for(i=0;i<size;i++)
{
 for(j=0;j<size-i-1;j++)
 {
```

```
if(name[j]>name[j+1]) //just replace > by < for descending order.
{
temp=name[j];
name[j]=name[j+1];
name[j+1]=temp;`
 }

 }
}
cout<<"\nAccending order is:";
for(i=0;i<size;i++)
{
cout<<" "<<name[i];
}
getch();
 }
```

References

1) http://freevideolectures.com/Course/2514/C++-Programming

2) http://www.learnerstv.com/video/Free-video-Lecture-13722-Computer-Science.htm

3) http://www.learnerstv.com/video/Free-video-Lecture-13723-Computer-Science.htm

4) http://www.learnerstv.com/video/Free-video-Lecture-13724-Computer-Science.htm

5) http://www.learnerstv.com/video/Free-video-Lecture-13725-Computer-Science.htm

6) http://www.learnerstv.com/video/Free-video-Lecture-13726-Computer-Science.htm

7) http://www.learnerstv.com/video/Free-video-Lecture-13727-Computer-Science.htm

8) http://www.learnerstv.com/video/Free-video-Lecture-13728-Computer-Science.htm

9) http://www.learnerstv.com/video/Free-video-Lecture-13738-Computer-Science.htm

10) http://youtube.com/watch?v=mZ1R-nFSWlE

11) http://youtube.com/watch?v=salHjct-H-Q

12) http://youtube.com/watch?v=-VW3OF11bFM

13) http://youtube.com/watch?v=JxpefLK-iPg

14) http://youtube.com/watch?v=a1k1lX1tv7s

(video Links)

1. https://www.youtube.com/watch?v=DYZxsW1eAqA

2. https://www.youtube.com/watch?v=M4E6CDkaMds

3. https://www.youtube.com/watch?v=mGy2s1hdqhk

4. https://www.youtube.com/watch?v=hSS0_yj9yBo

5. https://www.youtube.com/watch?v=vz1O9nRyZaY

6. http://www.studytonight.com/courses/cpp-video-tutorial/

7. https://www.youtube.com/watch?v=NYRhI0ivcR8

8. https://www.youtube.com/watch?v=gUFJW9Bmu-k

Video link From Chapter 1 to 4 (FCPIT)

1) https://www.youtube.com/results?search_query=intro+to+c%2B%2B+tutorials

2) https://www.youtube.com/watch?v=SWZfFNyUsxc&index=2&list=PLAE85DE8440AA6B83

3) https://www.youtube.com/results?search_query=c%2B%2B+tutorials

4) https://www.youtube.com/watch?v=tvC1WCdV1XU&list=PLAE85DE8440AA6B83

5) https://www.youtube.com/watch?v=S3t-5UtvDN0

6) https://www.youtube.com/watch?v=fy4hJWctkNc&index=12&list=PLfVsf4Bjg79Cu5MYkyJ-u4SyQmMhFeC1C

7) https://www.google.com/#q=c%2B%2B+tutorials+video+links

8) http://www.pvtuts.com/cpp/cpp-introduction

1) https://www.youtube.com/results?search_query=intro+to+c%2B%2B+tutorials

2) https://www.youtube.com/watch?v=SWZfFNyUsxc&index=2&list=PLAE85DE8440AA6B83

3) https://www.youtube.com/results?search_query=c%2B%2B+tutorials

4) https://www.youtube.com/watch?v=tvC1WCdV1XU&list=PLAE85DE8440AA6B83

5) https://www.youtube.com/watch?v=S3t-5UtvDN0

6) https://www.youtube.com/watch?v=fy4hJWctkNc&index=12&list=PLfVsf4Bjg79Cu5MYkyJ-u4SyQmMhFeC1C

7) https://www.google.com/#q=c%2B%2B+tutorials+video+links

8) http://www.pvtuts.com/cpp/cpp-introduction

AUTHOR'S PROFILE

Prof. Vijay Kumar Sinha   **Associate Professor**   Chandigarh Engineering College, Landran. Mohali.   Punjab, India PIN-140307   Mobile: 9781552900   Email:vijay.appsci@cgc.edu.in , cecm.cse.vk@gmail.com

Name   : **Vijay Kumar Sinha**

Father's Name   : Mahendra Prasad Sinha

Mother's Name   : **Kalindi Devi**

Designation   : Associate Professor

Present Work Place   : **Chandigarh Engineering College, Landran, Mohali (Punjab) India PIN-140307**

Research Scholar   : **Ph.D. under University (Affiliated to IKG Punjab technical University, Kapurthala , Punjab, India)**

Date of birth   : 05 Feb 1970

Qualifications   : Ph.D. (Computer Science & Engineering)

Address   : Chandigarh Engineering College, Landran (Mohali)-140307, Punjab, India.

Experience   : Teaching: 15 Years

Awards:

1.   Best Teacher Award at CGC, 2013

2.   Best Paper Award 2017 ICIC, Dec,2017

Paper Publications:

INTERNATIONAL JOURNALS (13):

1.   Vijay Kumar Sinha, Anuj Kumar Gupta, Mahajan Mahajan "Detecting fake iris in iris bio-metric system", Digital Investigation (2018), https://doi.org/10.1016/j.diin.2018.03.002, Elsevier Publication (SCI indexed).

2.   Vijay Kumar Sinha, Dr. Anuj Kumar Gupta, Dr. Ravinder Khanna "Detection of fake

Iris by Using frame Difference and Reflection Ratio", I J C T A, 9(41), pp. 1096-1102, Dec 2016 (SCOPUS)

3. Vijay Kumar Sinha, Dr. Ravinder Khanna and Dr. Manish Pandey, "Enhancing Security and Intelligence of Iris Recognition System" IJSTM, Vol.-4, Issue -2, Sep. 2013.

4. Vijay Kumar Sinha , Dr. Ravinder Khanna and Dr. Manish Pandey, "Detection and Filtration of Fake iris Images by Analyzing its Dynamic and Natural Movement Features" , IJSTM, Vol. 3 Issue 3 , July 2013.

5. Vijay Kumar Sinha, Dr. Anuj Gupta, Dr. Ravinder Khanna, Dr. Manish Mahajan "Enhancing iris security by detection of fake iris", National Conference Gyan Jyoti – National Conference MITE 2016.

6. Vijay Kumar Sinha, Dr. Anuj Kumar Gupta, Dr. Ravinder Khanna, Dr. Manish Mahajan "Authentication of Real Iris Images by Detection of Parallel Eyelid Blinks on Both Eyes" ICIC2017, Circulation in Computer Science, ISSN: 2456-3692, Dec 2017.

7. Vijay Kumar Sinha, Dr. Anuj Kumar Gupta "Detection of Iris Dilation on Both Eyes, As a Potential Biomarker for Fake Iris Detection" " ICIC2017, Circulation in Computer Science, ISSN: 2456-3692, Dec 2017

8. Vijay Kumar Sinha, Gurpreet Kaur "Analysis and Comparison of Mutants Reduction Techniques", Universal Journal of Management & Information Technology, Volume 1, Number 2. May 2016.

9. Vijay Kumar Sinha , " Reduction of Cost while Maintaining High Customer's Satisfaction by Using CBSE Software", International Journal of Innovative Research in Computer and Communication Engineering, Vol. 4, Issue 4, April 2016

10. Vijay Kumar Sinha, Mohita Narang "GCBSEEUC: A New Technique to Compute Energy Consumption in CBSE Software", IJIRCCE, Vol. 4, Issue 6, June 2016.

11. Vijay Kumar Sinha ,Rubaljeet Kaur, "Reduction of Cyclomatic Complexity by use of Mutation Testing", IJIRCCE, Vol. 4, Issue 4, April 2016.

12. Vijay Kumar Sinha, Dr. Anuj Kumar Gupta, Dr. Manish Mahajan , "Examining Iris Consciousness for Validation of Legal Contracts " , "International Conference on Innovations in Computing (ICIC2018)" .

13. Vijay Kumar Sinha, Dr. Anuj Kumar Gupta, Dr. Manish Mahajan , "Detection of Criminal Traces during Forced Iris Authentication" , "International Conference on Innovations in Computing (ICIC2018)" .

CONFERENCES (10):

1. Vijay Kumar Sinha , Dr. Anuj Kumar Gupta Dr. Ravinder Khanna," Detection of fake Iris by Using frame Difference and Reflection Ratio" , SCESM 2017 , SCOPUS Indexed International Conference , Jain College , Belagavi (Near Goa),India (Paper accepted ,Paper ID : 289).

2. Vijay Kumar Sinha, Dr. Anuj Gupta, "Enhancing iris security by detection of fake iris", National Conference Gyan Jyoti –National Conference MITE 2016.

3. Vijay Kumar Sinha, Dr. Anuj Kumar Gupta, Dr. Ravinder Khanna, Dr. Manish Mahajan "Detection of Iris Dilation on Both Eyes, as a Potential Biomarker for Fake Iris Detection" International Conference on Innovations in Computing (ICIC2017)" to be held on 14 December, 2017 organized by Department of Computer Science and Engineering, CGC College of Engineering, Chandigarh Group of Colleges, Mohali, Punjab, India.

4. Vijay Kumar Sinha, Dr. Anuj Kumar Gupta, Dr. Ravinder Khanna, Dr. Manish Mahajan, "Authentication of Real Iris Images by Detection of Parallel Eyelid Blinks on Both Eyes ", International Conference on Innovations in Computing (ICIC2017)" to be held on 15 December, 2017 organized by Department of Computer Science and Engineering, CGC College of Engineering, Chandigarh Group of Colleges, Mohali, Punjab, India.

5. Vijay Kumar Sinha, Dr. Anuj Kumar Gupta, Dr. Manish Mahajan (ICIC 2018) , "Examining Iris Consciousness for Validation of Legal Contracts " , "2nd International Conference on Innovations in Computing (ICIC2018)" organized by Department of Computer Science and Engineering, CGC College of Engineering, Chandigarh Group of Colleges, Mohali, Punjab, India.

6. Vijay Kumar Sinha, Dr. Anuj Kumar Gupta, Dr. Manish Mahajan (ICIC 2018) , "Detection of Criminal Traces during Forced Iris Authentication" , "2nd International Conference on Innovations in Computing (ICIC2018)" organized by Department of Computer Science and Engineering, CGC College of Engineering, Chandigarh Group of Colleges, Mohali, Punjab, India.

7. Vijay Kumar Sinha, (RTICCN, 2015), "Reducing Theoretical Complexity Metric for Component Based Softwares" , National Conference on "Recent Trends in Cloud Computing & Networking" , 26-27 March , 2015 , CGCCOE , Landran , Mohali, Punjab.

8. Vijay Kumar Sinha, "National Conference on Animation Perspectives ", A New Approach in Transition Based Animation Graphics for Statistical Data" at Indo Global College of Engineering, Abhipur, Mohali, Punjab.

9. Vijay Kumar Sinha ," An Improved Video Based Face Recognition System Including 3D Aging and Facial Marks ", 2nd International Conference "Srijan10", on Innovative Practices in Management & Information Technology for Excellence , Maharaja Agrasen Institute of Management & Technology , Jagadhri, 8 May 2010.

10. Vijay Kumar Sinha , Geet Kiran Kaur , Regional Student Convention 2010 on Trans disciplinary Computer Applications and Design Challenges, 21-22 October, 2010, By Computer Society of India at Chandigarh Engineering College, Landran, Mohali, Punjab.

Awards:

1. Best Teacher Award at CGC, Landran 2013

2.   Best Paper Award 2017 ICIC, Dec,2017

Books: 03

1. Enhancing Security & Intelligence of Iris Recognition System,

ISBN 978-613-9-98718-4 Lambert Academic Publishing, 2018

2. Enhancement of Security in Iris Recognition System by Luster Detection,

ISBN 978-613-9-98958-4 , Lambert Academic Publishing , 2018

3. Enhancement of Degraded Text Images & Performance Comparisons, ISBN 978-613-9-99926-2 , Lambert Academic Publishing , 2019

Rubal Jeet
Assistant Professor
Chandigarh Engineering ,
Landran, Mohali
Research Scholar , Chandigarh University , Ghruan,
Mohali, Punjab, India
rubaljeet.2050@cgc.edu.in

Rubaljeet received her M.Tech. degree in Computer Science and Engineering from IKG Punjab Technical University, Kapurthala (India) .She is a research scholar at Chandigar University , Ghruan , Mohali(Punjab). She is currently working at Chandigarh Engineering College, Landran, Mohali (Punjab). Her research interests includes Body Area Wireless Sensor Network , Biometric Security etc. She is teaching C & C++ since 10 years for engineering graduate students . She is a pursuing Ph.D. program from Chandigarh University , Mohali in Wireless Baody Sensor Area Network. She published a number of research papers in reffered journals.

Meenakshi Jaiswal
meenakshi.1233@cgc.edu.in
Assistant Professor
Chandigarh Engineering College,
Landran,
Mohali (Punjab)
PIN 140307
India

Ms. Meenakshi Jaiswal is working as Assistant Professor at Chandigarh Engineering college , Landran , Mohali (Punjab) , under IKG-PTU . She is M.Tech. in Computer Science & Engineering . She is teaching C & C++ since 10 years to under graduate engineering students . Her area of research interest includes software engineering , Software reuse , Green Computing and big data. She published a number of research papers in reffered journals.